Forgotten Fields
of America

VOLUME THREE

Forgotten Fields
of America

VOLUME THREE

World War II Bases and Training, then and now.

Typography and design: Kitty Herrin, Arrow Graphics

Unless noted, all photographs are by the author.

Library of Congress Catalog Card No. 96-69800

ISBN 1-57510-102-5

First Printing: June 2003

PICTORIAL HISTORIES PUBLISHING COMPANY, INC.
713 South Third Street West, Missoula, Montana 59801
Phone (406) 549-8488   Fax (406) 728-9280
email: phpc@montana.com

Contents

Title page photo: Dick Schneider at Ridgewell, England (Station 167), when he was nearing the end of his tour. Dick flew a total of 28 missions, 26 as a B-17 tail gunner over Europe.

Acknowledgments

THE BEST PART OF WRITING these books is meeting the wonderful people who lived the history. They represent the greatness of America, and it is a privilege for me to know them.

Thanks so much to my wife, Jane, for her patience and help with this book and the two others that preceded it. Her constant encouragement, ideas, and suggestions for improvement made this a better book. My daughter, Elizabeth, poured over each chapter, and it's because of her work that they are in readable form. My older son, David, was PIC on several trips. We always managed to arrive at the right place and at the right time. My younger son, Chip, took the time to accompany me to two of the former Air Force bases. His company was most welcome.

I owe a special debt of gratitude to the United States Air Force, and the folks of the 14th Flying Training Wing at Columbus Air Force Base for allowing me the opportunity to observe the training of today's Air Force pilots. Special thanks to Ms. Connie Lisowski, Captain Timothy Sundvall, and 1st Lt. Joseph Coslett.

The starting point for researching the history of most of the bases in this volume is the microfilm records held at the Air Force Historical Research Agency, Maxwell AFB, Alabama. I especially want to thank Ms. Essie Roberts for her kindness and help locating these records, and her advice on those pertinent to my needs. I am also very appreciative of the assistance given me by Messrs. Joseph Caver and Dennis Case with the Tuskegee Airmen research.

Finally, I was privileged to meet many special people who helped with my research through their sharing of memories, photos, memorabilia, and who patiently answered my questions. I am in their debt. Many thanks to: Gale Ammerman, Wally Baldwin, Larry Barnett, Dr. Caesar Bassette, John Becket, Fr. Joseph Beckman, Dr. Blair Bentley, Norman Berge, Tim Bivens, Thomas Bradbury, Brian Carr, Herbert Carter, Cecil Caudill, Adele Cohill, Lemuel Custis, Don Doram, Charles Dunn, Dr. David Fellinger, Trent Ferrell, Doug Gentry, Bill Guyton, Lenore Hafley, Patsy Hamer, Dr. Lawrence Hawkins, Mr. and Mrs. Alan Henry, Wes Henry, Pat Higdon, June Hinkle, Randy Hoffman, Lyle Hopkins, Earl Horton, Mike Horton, John Hoza, Curtis Hubbard, Char Jackson, Mike Jordan, Ted Jordan, Tom Kelly, Eva LaRue, Malinda Lawrence, John Leahr, Harry Lee, Paul London, Don Klinko, Tom MacCullum, Lille McKay, Lonna McKinley, P.J. McLaughlin, David McPheeters, John McRae, Allen Metscher, Godfrey Miller, Monte Monroe, Lt. Jennifer Moore, Stan Mulsford, Nicholas Neblett, Merle Olmsted, Dr. Julian Peasant, Jim Petersen, Mack Pong, Jimmy Porter, Dean Reno, Jerry Rep, David Runyan, Bob Sanford, Dick Schneider, Robert Schultz, Tommy Simmons, Ann Slaughter, George Swift, George Theis, Dr. Winston Tornow, Bill Tynan, Eric Williams, Gen. Clinton Willis Jr., Viola Whipperman, Ray White, Wayne Wong, and Gen. Chuck Yeager.

Foreword

IN WRITING THREE VOLUMES on America's World War II training bases, Lou Thole has created a pleasant irony in that "forgotten fields" are no longer forgotten. Instead, they are brought to life again with vivid storytelling and imagery that meaningfully connects past and present. Lou's series provides an important look back at a rapidly vanishing but very important part of the Air Force story.

This third volume deals with bases that are probably familiar to readers of a certain generation: Columbus, Dyersburg, Kingman, Laurinburg-Maxton, Page, Reese, Tonopah, Tuskegee, Venice, Wendover, and Williams. If these names are unfamiliar to younger readers, this points out the central value of this kind of book. These chronicles help to make sense of local scenes and landscapes, surrounded by legend and rumor, that perhaps live only or mostly in the memories of the people who lived the bases' stories—and those people are unfortunately growing fewer.

Lou has delved into what really happened in these places, and he keeps alive the stories of real people's work and sacrifices. The core meaning of Lou's project is evident in this volume, and that is the idea that while landscapes change and evolve, human stories connected with them can and should be saved for the sake of knowledge. Knowing what sort of people worked so hard at these old bases, and understanding why they did it, is key in appreciating the local history set out in these books. No less important, it's also an effective way to understand, honor and preserve Air Force heritage and culture.

The *Forgotten Fields* series is a notable achievement in bringing together many diverse stories and sources into one accessible, focused project. As you absorb these compelling stories, the scenes of historic events will become doubly meaningful, either in enriching your memories of these bases, or satisfying the urge to know "what happened here, and why."

—CHARLES D. METCALF, *Major General, USAF (Ret)*
Director, United States Air Force Museum

Introduction

I WROTE THIS BOOK and the two that preceded it to tell a story that is largely forgotten in the history of the United States Air Force. Actually, it's a story within a story, one that takes place during the finest and most difficult period in American history. It is a magnificent chapter in our past because of the results achieved when Americans came together as never before to face and defeat a common enemy. Starting virtually from scratch, and largely unencumbered by governmental red tape, partisan politics, and with a strong belief in God; Americans built the foundation for the greatest aerial force the world has ever seen.

In 1939, most of America was just waking up to the threat to its freedom, and would soon learn again that, "Freedom Is Not Free." At best, the Air Force (Air Corps) in 1939 was little more than a second string operation, with excellent leadership, but owned its existence to the whims of an isolationist congress. At the time, there were just 17 air bases and few combat ready aircraft. In 1938, there were just two training fields, (Randolph and Kelly) and their training capacity was about 500 pilots per year.

Into the breech stepped Major General Henry H. Arnold, who as newly appointed Chief of the U.S. Air Corps put into operation a building and training program, the scope of which was unprecedented. In just a few years there would be a total of 783 airfields, most of which sprang up during 1941 and 1942. Not all were complete installations. Some were subbases, and others were auxiliary landing fields. These training centers would graduate 224,331 pilots, over 46,000 navigators, more than 42,000 bombardiers, and 282,836 gunners.

It is difficult today to imagine how fast and well these new training centers were built. Within a period of a few months (normally six) a major training center would spring up where just a short time before there was nothing but empty fields or wooded land. Thousands of workers would travel to the new building site, and finding accommodations where they could (some lived in tents, dormitories converted from existing buildings, and rooms rented from local residents), they set about to build the base.

Civilian contractors did the work with oversight by a few officers and men of the Corps of Engineers. Standards were high, and the use of initiative and local decision making was encouraged. Speed was of the essence. To compensate for the weather, one field had its runways put down under the protection of circus tents; another contractor went into an abandoned mine to take up the railroad tracks. He did not have the time to wait for his order to be filled. One Corps of Engineers Officer needing fireplugs and realizing he was too far down on the list to wait for them, simply sent out a truck at night to the manufacturer's facility. His men cut through the fence and took them. He left a check in payment. Others improvised as they could to meet a demanding time timetable, and the fields were built. And to their credit, many of the runways are still used today, as are some of the buildings that they so hastily put up.

There were 345 major bases, most of which were used to train the pilots, navigators, gunners, mechanics, radio operators and bombardiers so desperately needed. Each of these bases was a small self-contained town with about 400 buildings, and three runways each about a mile long. The structures were generally temporary in nature, and called "Theatre of Operations" buildings. They were made of wood, tar paper, and non-masonry siding. Concrete and steel were seldom used because of their need elsewhere. These buildings, with the possible exception of the hospital, had no insulation, the outside walls were siding nailed to a two by four stud. Air-conditioning was unknown, and heat was provided by one or two small stoves fueled by coal. These structures were bitterly cold in the winter, and provided no protection from the heat and dust of summer.

Normally the bases were built in sparsely populated areas, often near a small town. The base population that ran into the thousands often exceeded that of the nearby town. While this situation created an economic boom for the nearby communities, it also caused serious problems. One of these problems was housing for the civilian workers on the base, the loved ones of those taking training, and those who were permanently stationed at the training center. Often, workers and married soldiers assigned to the base were able to rent a room, sometimes at an exorbitant rate, in a home in the nearby town. These were the lucky ones. Others were forced to live in converted chicken coops, barns, one room shacks, and on one base, the upstairs of the local jail. The housing problem, while addressed by the military, was never satisfactory solved. It all happened too fast.

With the war's end most of these once thriving bases became unwanted and unused. For a brief period of time they were ghost towns, quiet and deserted. Only a few caretakers were left to protect the property against fire, vandalism, and perform critical maintenance. No meals were served in the mess halls, classrooms were empty, drill fields began to sprout weeds, and the flag no longer flew over base headquarters. "No Trespassing" signs went up as the government slowly went through the process of selling off or giving the property back to the taxpayers.

Probably the most complete World War II training base remaining is Wendover Field, Utah. Its story is told in this book. Other "temporary fields" and buildings are still in place, scattered across the United States. Some are derelict and abandoned, the long concrete runways and remains of building foundations slowly being concealed by weeds and brush. Some have been converted into industrial parks, where the concrete runways have made excellent building foundations. A few still serve as active Air Force installations, or busy civilian airports.

Why I Want To Be A Pilot

When I grow up I want to be a pilot because it's a fun job and easy to do. That's why there are so many pilots flying around these days.

Pilots don't need much school. They just have to learn to read numbers so they can read their instruments. I guess they should be able to read a road map too.

Pilots should be brave so they won't get scared if it's foggy and they can't see, or if a wing or motor falls off.

Pilot should have to have good eyes to see through the clouds, and they can't be afraid of thunder or lightning because they are much closer to them than we are.

The salary pilots make is another thing I like. They make more money than they know what to do with. This is because most people think that flying a plane is dangerous, except pilots don't because they know how easy it is.

I hope I don't get air-sick because I get car-sick and if I get air-sick I couldn't be a pilot and then I would have to go to work.

—WRITTEN BY A FIFTH GRADER

Taken from the *Euro NATO Joint Jet Pilot Training* class book, Class 90-07

Captain Roy Morse teaching cadets how to send and receive code, January 1942.
(AIR FORCE HISTORICAL RESEARCH AGENCY)

1
The Experiment

TUSKEGEE ARMY AIR FIELD

In 1940, some said the decision to train African-Americans to fly high performance fighter aircraft was an "experiment designed to fail." Regardless, the program proved to be a magnificent success and was important to the acceptance of blacks into the mainstream of aviation. Tuskegee Army Airfield would graduate the first black-Americans ever to wear the wings of a pilot in the United States Air Force.

One of the major problems facing the successful development of training at Tuskegee Army Air Field was racial prejudice. Today it is difficult for many people to comprehend the second class citizen status of the African-American in the United States during the 1940s. This was the atmosphere that prevailed when the decision was made to train a group of African-American men to become pilots in the U.S. Army Air Corps, later renamed the United States Army Air Forces. Prior to this time, it was impossible for a black man to be accepted for pilot training in any branch of the U.S. Military. The decision to accept (on an extremely limited basis) was forced by the black press, black leaders, and a few farsighted whites with political influence. The Air Corps leader at the time, General Arnold stated, in a 1940 memo, that blacks could be used "in labor battalions or labor companies to perform

the duties of post fatigue and as waiters in our messes." The memo also stated "Negro pilots cannot be used in our present Air Corps units since this would result in having Negro officers serving over white enlisted men. This would create an impossible social problem." General Arnold's statement was a reflection of society as it existed in 1940.

Tuskegee Army Air Field would be just like any other Air Corps training field, yet it would be unique. It was segregated and unwanted. The field was located on about 1,650 acres about seven air miles northwest of the small rural town of Tuskegee Alabama. At the time the population of Tuskegee was about 4,000 people and most of the white citizens were not happy with the building of a "colored" training facility near their town. In his autobiography, *Benjamin O Davis Jr. American*, a retired four star general, and the first black officer to earn his wings in the Air Force called Tuskegee "a hick town." Key citizens complained that building the field would hurt the town economically because it would block expansion of the town in that direction. Actually, most cities pleaded for an air base near their town because of the significant positive economic impact of the thousands of workers and military men and women. This was

1

Aerial photo of Tuskegee Army Air Field as it was in July 1945. (AIR FORCE MUSEUM)

not to be the case with Tuskegee Army Air Field.

During its service, the field would have three names: Air Corps Advanced Flying School, Tuskegee Army Flying School, and finally, Tuskegee Army Air Field. The decision to build at Tuskegee was more complicated than other training fields because of the race issue. In addition to other considerations, there was considerable disagreement among African-Americans about the question of segregated versus integrated training. The NAACP along with others including Judge William Hastie, the civilian aide to Secretary of War Henry L. Stinson, believed the training should be integrated. Judge Hastie felt so strongly about this that on January 31,

1943 he resigned in protest of segregated training. Others, including Dr. Patterson, president of Tuskegee Institute, felt the training, even if segregated, was a step in the right direction and would open the doors for further advancement for African-Americans.

The selection sites were narrowed down to Tuskegee, Alabama and Chicago, Illinois. There was a large African-American training field in Chicago—The Coffey School of Aeronautics. Some key factors in the decision to locate at Tuskegee were the more favorable weather, the heavy aerial traffic in the Chicago area, and the already in place Primary training field (Moton Field). Also located in Tuskegee were a Veterans

2

Overhead view of the cantonment area of Tuskegee Army Air Field, June 1945. Of interest is the circle roadway in the center of the cantonment area, this was the site of the post headquarters. The housing area in the upper right corner is Mitchell Village. (AIR FORCE MUSEUM)

Administration hospital and the Tuskegee Institute (Tuskegee University), a premier educational facility for blacks.

Fort Davis, Alabama, about fourteen miles south of the city of Tuskegee, was one of the final sites considered but was rejected because of soil conditions that would require extensive work to make the area suitable for an airfield. On April 30, 1941 the site selection board met and inspected the area that would later become the location of the Tuskegee Army Air Field. Later the land was acquired from eight property owners with the total cost being $74,549.58. The area was a combination of woods and farmland with the main crop being cotton. Some of the land was level and required only minimal preparation prior to building; however, the northern part of the airfield was hilly which required extensive grading and the removal of trees. There were several streams on the land and one (the Uphapee Creek) had to have its channel changed in order to build the base. Hilyard Robinson of Washington would design the field and the prime contractor was McKissack & McKissack of Nashville, Tennessee. Both firms were African-American.

Construction began on July 12, 1941 with the removal of trees. The leveling of the land started later in the month. The base was no where near completion in November when training

Two photos taken in 1996 give a current view of the field. Note the circle roadway (site of the post headquarters), the road system, ramp, and runways.

started. The first cadets used the only runway—the north/south runway—even though it was not finished. It had been graded but not paved. At the time training started, the administration and housing were just one third completed and the hospital building was about 65% complete. As a result, the early arrivals lived in very primitive conditions.

By September 1943, the field had approximately 225 buildings and four runways. The base had no auxiliary field of its own when training started. Later, the first auxiliary field, Tallassee Field, was built. It was renamed Griel Auxiliary Field, after the original landowner of the bulk of the property. This field had a total of about 325 acres and was located about six miles west of the main base. At first, it was not usable in wet weather.

The first commander of Tuskegee Army Air Field was Major Ellison, who took command in late July 1941. Prior to this, he had served as the field's project officer. His major contribution was to get the field in some kind of condition to begin training in November. As a result, he was very involved in the construction phase and did not spend as much time as he would have liked handling administration detail. As a result, organization suffered. This is understandable in view of the lack of trained personnel, equipment, housing, and the wet weather that turned the area into a mud puddle. Major Ellison also faced the problem of local prejudice. As an example, when Major Ellison replaced the white civilian watchman with military personnel, the base history reports "some of the civilians called on the Post Commander (Major Ellison) and objected strenuously and in a threatening manner to being replaced by Negro personnel." In his book *Segregated Skies*, author Stanley Sandler writes: "Ellison, as noted, had been enthusiastic about the Tuskegee program—He was a decent, sincere, blunt old pilot who had apparently even opposed some of the segregation policies prevailing in surrounding Macon County."

Major Ellison remained with the field through start up of training and was replaced by Col. Frederick Kimble in January 1942. Although Col. Kimble's stay at the field was short (about a year), the role he played was crucial. He got the field up and running, and through his contacts with Washington was able to secure badly needed supplies on an expedited basis. He is not remembered fondly by the blacks who served at Tuskegee Army Air Field. The Colonel was a strict segregationist and insured the field would resemble society as a whole which at the time was segregated. As a result, Col. Kimble insisted on separate facilities for the blacks and whites including the posting of "white" and "colored" signs for the various facilities. This situation was not made easier by the negative reporting that he received in the black newspapers, which at the time, were very influential along with other groups opposed to the field's segregated status.

By 1942, it had been decided the field would play a much larger role than first imagined. The idea that the station would be a small flying school and base for the all black 99th Pursuit Squadron was changed soon after the bombing of Pearl Harbor. The base was under the jurisdiction of the Flying Training Command, but eventually would have units from the Technical Training Command, the Air Service Command, and the Third Air Force. It was up to the post commander to house and feed the units even though they were not under the command of the Flying Training Command. This caused considerable problems for Col. Kimble. By the end of 1942, Tuskegee Army Air Field had a total of 3,414 men, 67 of whom

Four aircraft that were used for training at Moton Field and Tuskegee AAF. At the top is a PT-17 primary trainer, next is a BT-13 basic trainer, then the AT-6 used for advanced training, and finally a P-40 used in transition training. (AIR FORCE HISTORICAL RESEARCH AGENCY)

were white. It was the only USAAF training field that taught Basic, Advanced, and Transition training at the same location.

In order to meet the quotas required by the War Department that all branches of the military must take at least ten percent of its total from the black population, many black units were created and then assigned to Tuskegee. As a result, Tuskegee Army Air Field often became a dumping ground for black units formed but not wanted at the other stations. Even though the headquarters at Tuskegee was responsible for administration of the units, those units would

5

Cadets in rigid meal time posture preparing to eat. Note the Spartan furnishings that were typical of the temporary buildings of the day. (AIR FORCE HISTORICAL RESEARCH AGENCY)

receive orders from their headquarters not located at the base. Also, the field received many black officer graduates from the Army Air Forces Officer Candidate School because higher headquarters did not know what to do with them. By the end of 1944, the officer/enlisted men ratio was about one officer to every five enlisted men. In addition, sometimes orders were issued to units at Tuskegee without the prior knowledge of the Tuskegee headquarters. To make matters even more interesting, some commands were confused as to what was located at Tuskegee Army Air Field. This was all in addition to the normal problems associated with a major training facility. The early history of the field notes "—the majority of troops on the station know that their presence in the Air Forces is permitted reluctantly and that they are a source of embarrassment to the War Department." David McPheeters was a student officer in Class 44-I who had washed out of Primary. Speaking about the general mix of

people at Tuskegee AAF, he said that he "was absolutely amazed at the number of educated and intelligent black men and women, had never seen that before . . . had high test scores . . . saw all these men with college degrees learning to fly, even enlisted men . . . it was sure flattering for me to be there."

Charles E. Francis gives a good example of part of the problem in his book, *The Tuskegee Airmen*. He writes: "In the spring of 1944 Colonel Parrish called an assembly to introduce the officer personnel of the field. There were assistants galore, assistant to the assistant Mess officer, assistant to the assistant Supply officer, assistant to this, to that, and even assistants to a makeshift position as Post Beautification officer—so many, in fact that it was actually humiliating. Those who had gone through the rigors of training at the various officers' training schools felt useless and despondent. . . . Many members of the 99th Fighter Squadron and the

Cadets being led in physical training by Sgt. Sablo. One Tuskegee Airman recalls "he would ruin you especially with Rifle Calisthenics. He took no prisoners, officers and enlisted men alike." (AIR FORCE HISTORICAL RESEARCH AGENCY)

332nd Fighter Group found Tuskegee a very disheartening place when they returned from combat. Though they had risked their lives fighting for their country they were given no assignment to keep them occupied." The book goes on to note that even Colonel Roberts, the former commander of the 99th Fighter Squadron and the 332nd Fighter Group, was treated in the same degrading manner: "He was assigned as a Bachelor Quarters officer, a position that the lowest non-commissioned officer could have held."

By the end of 1942, there were 121 cadets taking flying training at Tuskegee in addition to the training of the 99th Fighter Squadron, the 332nd Fighter Group, the 96th Service Group and perhaps other units. To quote the official history: "That confusion reigned supreme will not be denied by anyone stationed here during this period . . ."

Perhaps Col. Noel Parrish, who succeeded Col. Kimble in December 1942, said it best in the Forward to the base history: ". . . Tuskegee Army Air Field was conceived as a working solution to the problem of training Negro Pilots for the United States Army Air Forces. Before the plans for the field were complete, it had already become the subject of considerable controversy and many differences of opinion. The

purpose of the field made it a focal point for one of the major social and governmental problems of the nation. There existed no precedent, no set of customs, no established procedures to guide military men in their efforts to build a functioning military organization in the midst of endless theorizing and uninformed discussion concerning racial characteristics and social proprieties. . . . The air field became a concentrated training center within itself, with functions and operations so diverse that no higher command staff could ever completely understand the nature and variety of its problems. Not only were flying units trained, organized and sent direct to combat, but signal corps units, quartermaster cadres, service units, and other assorted organizations were housed, organized, trained, processed and finally dispatched from this station. All of these things were accomplished without interference with the field's primary function—to train pilots."

Col. Parrish was the man on whose shoulders fell the responsibility to make sense of this and to insure that the primary mission of training was achieved. Prior to assuming command of the field, Col. Parrish was director of Basic Training and organized the Basic and Advanced training programs. He is remembered fondly by the men and women who served at Tuskegee.

Col. Parrish was a Southerner who went out of his way to understand and help the black personnel face the additional roadblocks created by segregation. He believed they were every bit as capable as whites, and was determined they be given the opportunity to prove so. One of the first graduates, Rodney Custis wrote to the author and said ". . . In your comments about the progress and development of TAAF, there is one person deserving mention—he is Noel F. Parrish who became the C.O. of TAAF. He was the glue that kept the project together." John Leahr, Class 43-G remembers, "Col. Parrish joined the Tuskegee Airmen Inc. organization as soon as it was formed in 1972 and was the speaker at their first convention. He was the only white officer from TAAF to join the organization. Col. Parrish never missed a convention of the organization until he became ill." The field would always have an air of segregation, but under Col. Parrish it was not aggressively pursued. Instead he went out of his way to speak at Rotary Club meetings at Tuskegee and Tallassee to help build understanding and support for the training center.

Rodney Custis was in the historic first group of cadets (class 42-C) to train at Tuskegee and was also in the original group of thirteen to enter primary flight training at Moton Field. He recalls: "At the time, there was just one runway, and we had to live in tents for awhile. That was no hard-ship when you are twenty and were achieving your dream of learning to fly. The tents were close to the field and had no facilities; we drank out of a water bag and had no hot or cold running water. The conditions were primitive; barracks, runways, technical facilities and utilities were not completed at the time training started. Training took place wherever possible, in partially completed buildings, in tents, and out of doors. Meals were eaten in an open tent with a dirt floor. There were no sanitary facilities. When the weather began to turn, the rain made the area a sea of mud. A simple tent facility housed the cadets, the mess hall, and a latrine. The first headquarters on the field was located in an old farm house and the farm building across the road was used as a supply building."

Since at first there were no black men trained in the areas necessary for an Air Corps training center (i.e. mechanics, weather, etc.), fifteen white enlisted men arrived on the site to help train the black enlisted men. The first white enlisted man, Sgt. Leroy Vanover, arrived on August 1, 1941. The first group of black support personnel (18 total) arrived on September 19, 1941 after being transferred from Maxwell Field, Alabama. They had previously finished technical training at Chanute Army Air Field in Illinois and were staying at Maxwell until being transferred to Tuskegee. Since there were no facilities ready on the field, they were quartered in a dormitory at

The day ends with a retreat ceremony, September 1942. (AIR FORCE HISTORICAL RESEARCH AGENCY)

The first class of black pilots to earn their wings in the U.S. Air Force gathered around their training plane with one of their instructors. From left to right: Charles DeBow Jr., Lemuel Custis, Mac Ross, Captain Benjamin O. Davis Jr., (seated in the aircraft) George Roberts, and the instructor Lt. R. M. Long. (AIR FORCE HISTORICAL RESEARCH AGENCY)

Tuskegee Institute. By early December, there was a total of 156 men on the field. A little after this, in January 1942, a group of 324 enlisted men of the 99th Pursuit Squadron and the air base detachment arrived on the field from Maxwell Field, Alabama. They had received their technical training at Chanute Field, and had been temporarily stationed at Maxwell awaiting facilities at Tuskegee. Eventually, five hundred black volunteers and six Aviation Cadets would receive their technical training at Chanute.

Four basic training planes (BT-13s) arrived on November 8, 1941, the same day the first class of cadets arrived. That was the official date

for the start of training the first class. The runway was not finished, and since there was only one runway, crosswind take offs and landings were common. The mess hall had a sand floor and the food was cooked over gasoline pump stoves. Water was boiled for drinking and cooking. The cadet's first uniform was khaki, with a black tie and black low quarter shoes. The Aviation cadet insignia was worn on the shirt collar and the flight cap.

The ground school started on November 10 in an unfinished barracks. There were four tents at the north end of the runway and they served as a parachute room, communications, cadet ready room, and supply and maintenance. Another group of tents housed all the enlisted personnel, cadets, a classroom, and an office for the school secretary. The group of tents was called Tent City or Camp Hazard in honor of the field's Executive Officer, Captain John T. Hazard. Among the first men to start flying training at Tuskegee Army Air Field were Captain Benjamin Davis Jr., Cadets Lemuel Custis, Charles DeBow, Frederick Moore, Jr., George Roberts, and Mac Ross. Cadet Moore, Jr. did not graduate, but the others did. They are the first blacks ever to earn their wings as members of the United States Air Force.

Initially, the ground school had four enlisted men as instructors along with a director. Subjects covered were Meteorology, Radio Code, Airplanes, Engines, Navigation, and Radio Communication. One of the first civilians to be hired as a ground school instructor was Dr. Caesar Bassette. A graduate of Hampton Institute (University), he had been accepted at Howard University medical school but at the time was teaching high school in Saint Louis. His mother told him "the government was looking for him" as part of a nationwide search for black instructors to teach Morse code at Tuskegee. He was one of the few blacks that knew Morse code and was also a certified teacher. After reporting to Tuskegee as a civilian instructor, he was later commissioned a 2nd Lieutenant by the base commander, Lt. Col. Noel Parrish. One of Caesar's early impressions of the field was that "nothing was paved, it was nothing but a mud hole down there." For a while, he lived with a family at the Tuskegee Institute campus. Each day the field would send a Jeep to the Institute to pick him up and take him to the base. Later on, he became Supervisor of Instructors of

One of the U.S.O. groups who entertained the troops at Tuskegee Army Air Field included Rochester and Leon Rene. Here they are shown signing autographs for patients at the base hospital during their visit.
(AIR FORCE HISTORICAL RESEARCH AGENCY)

Secretary of War Henry L. Stimson (with cane) is shown being greeted by Lt. Gen. Barton Yount, commander of the AAF Training Command upon his visit to the field. The photo includes Benjamin O. Davis Jr., but in fact he did not meet Stimson during his visit. To satisfy a request from the Pentagon, TAAF officials made a photo of Davis and superimposed his image on the photograph of Stimson's arrival, thus giving the impression that Davis had met the secretary while he was at Tuskegee AAF.

(AIR FORCE HISTORICAL RESEARCH AGENCY)

radio code and communications. He taught the first class (that included then Captain B.O. Davis, Jr.) and he was there when the base closed in 1946. One of his sad memories is of his best student who could take 15–25 code words per minute "... the student went out on a training flight one afternoon and never came back." He died in a training accident.

As time went by, the curriculum for the ground school was expanded and additional courses added. This was necessary because of added training responsibilities and the requirement to train men for other than flight training. By early 1944 the ground school, at Tuskegee Army Air Field was teaching Preflight, Basic, Advanced Single Engine, Advanced Twin Engine, Liaison, Bombardier-Navigation Preflight and some bombardier courses. Also a Post Technical School Building was constructed to train men in armament, radio operation and repair, aircraft mechanics, administrative and technical duties. No other training field handled such a complex and demanding variety of training responsibilities. The official history notes a comment by Captain Martin, Director of Ground School, about directives concerning Pre-Flight School. He notes "... that higher headquarters evidently forgets or is unaware of the numerous activities carried on at the field."

It should be pointed out that men were sent to other bases for special training. Some of the bases that trained men assigned to Tuskegee included: Camp Crowder, Lowry Field, Chanute Field, Kessler Field, Scott Field, Buckley Field, Atlanta University, and Lincoln Army Air Field. In effect, Tuskegee Army Air Field was serving as a classification center for all black personnel assigned to the Army Air Forces.

Following Basic flight training, the first class started Advanced training in January 1942. This course included Armament, Gunnery, Tactics and Technique of air fighting, Advanced Navigation, Maintenance, Engineering, and Employment of Aviation in the Army. By early 1944, there were thirteen flying instructors, and about 36 AT-6s used in the training. Each instructor had four or five students. Gunnery and combat tactics training was taken at Eglin Field, Florida where the first class arrived on February 23, 1942. It was in the Advanced phase of training that the first cadet, Robert A. Dawson from San Antonio, Texas, would lose his life during 1942.

At this point, in early to mid 1944, all flight instructors were white; however, black instructors were being phased into some parts of the flight training.

Godfrey Miller was in one of the later classes at Tuskegee, 45-H, and recalls that his class went directly from the primary trainer (PT-13) at Moton Field to the T-6 at Tuskegee. He recalls

11

Col. Noel F. Parrish, the Commanding Officer at Tuskegee Army Air Field, seen at his desk at post headquarters. He was highly respected by those who served at Tuskegee Army Air Field. He was outspoken in his efforts to ease the unfairness of segregation and was diligent in his attempts to gain acceptance for those who worked and trained on the base. (AIR FORCE MUSEUM)

that he "took to flying like a duck to water—never flunked a check ride." He still remembers his Basic Flying instructor, Flight Officer Gordon, "as a tough guy, who knew his business. If you didn't hack it, he would take the stick and slap it;" this would cause the stick to bang against the cadet's knees. Of his days at Tuskegee, he says "It was great, I enjoyed it. I was braced and hazed but that was all part of the game."

After advanced training, transition training began with old P-40s, the first of which arrived in April 1942 and caused considerable excitement. John Leahr remembers his transition training in the old P-40s: "The real challenge was to get 26 men through the course in two barely flyable P-40s. We were informed that in case of any trouble with the aircraft, to bail out immediately. One of the members, Maurice Page, had to bail when his plane caught fire. This left us with just one P-40

to finish the course." General Davis, a member of the first class, recalls in his book, Benjamin O Davis, Jr. American, of the war weary P-40s "every one of them leaking oil." The first cadet to save his life via parachute was Lt. Mac Ross, who bailed out of his P-40 during a training mission after trying to return to the field because his P-40 had smoke pouring from the engine.

As with all the other training fields, the training at Tuskegee was constantly changed and upgraded to take advantage of improved facilities and added courses.

An example of the complexity of the flying training challenge at Tuskegee is gained by looking at some of the different aircraft parts stored in the field's warehouses. As of December 1943, these included parts for the PT-17, PT-19, BT-13, AT-6, AT-10, P40, P-39, UC-78, Piper L-4, and the Taylorcraft L-2. Almost certainly to this list were added parts for the B-25 that would later be used for twin engine training. Some of these aircraft were probably not used for training at Tuskegee, such as the PT-17 and PT-19. These were flown at the Primary Field located at nearby Moton Field. Also the UC-78 was probably used for transportation. It is not known if the P-39 was ever used as a training aircraft at Tuskegee.

The attitude of the people of Tuskegee, the distance of the post from the town, coupled with the poor roads, and the limited entertainment facilities insured that there was little social life for the cadets and enlisted men. As of May 1941, Tuskegee had one hotel (43 rooms—whites only), a golf course for whites and one for blacks (Tuskegee Institute). Also, there was one theater, divided in half, one for whites, the other for blacks. There were three restaurants: one in the hotel (no evening meals, closed on Sunday) the Victory Tearoom (also closed on Sunday), and later a filling station converted into a restaurant. The blacks that first arrived at Tuskegee Army Air Field were able to take advantage of the recreational facilities at the Institute. These included a gymnasium, swimming pool, athletic fields, and a library. There were also free movies shown at the Tuskegee Veterans Facility. The town of Tuskegee made available the use of a tennis court,

This was the Post Headquarters building as it appeared late in the war. The first headquarters on the post was located in a farm building. (AIR FORCE MUSEUM)

a swimming pool, and some other recreational facilities to the white military personnel.

At best, the relationship between the town of Tuskegee, and the post was always strained. Adding to the problem was the fact that the black MPs from the post were armed during their town patrols. This caused considerable concern among many of the town people including the mayor who insisted the MPs only be equipped with nightsticks. Mistakes were made on both sides. The tension came to a head on April 1, 1942 when a military policeman took away a soldier from a city policeman at the point of a pistol. This action was in violation of military rules, and caused a near tragic incident. Eventually, the

MPs from Tuskegee Army Air Field entered the town armed only with nightsticks.

Some of the comments made by the men who trained at Tuskegee Army Air Field are indicative of the attitude of many living in the town. Dr. Lawrence Hawkins, who was a member of class 45-G, recalls that "Tuskegee had a black section and a white section. You didn't go into the white section . . . The police would pick you up and fine you for whatever you had in your pocket . . . so you had to be careful on payday." On one occasion he drove into a gas station in Tuskegee and had five gallons of gas put into his car. At the time, gas cost 25 cents per gallon. "I gave the gas station attendant a $5.00 bill. The attendant walked into the gas station, came out and started to read a newspaper. When I mentioned that he forgot to give me my change, the man went back into the building, got a 38 cal. pistol pressed it to my head and said 'nigger do

This photo shows the new barracks in the background with some of the tents that were used when the field first opened. (AIR FORCE MUSEUM)

you still want your change?' I said, 'that's OK, just keep the change'." Years later when he returned to Tuskegee for a visit, he noticed the same building was there but the gas station was gone. He thought about going in and asking for his change.

Don Doram class of 44-I felt no protection from the military. People could take your life and nothing could be done to prevent it. When he had time, he would spend his weekends in Atlanta or Birmingham, Alabama. Lt. Col. Godfrey Miller USAF (Ret.), class 45- H, had this to say about the town: "It just scared me. If someone were to challenge me, I was dead. I knew what I would not take." Nick Neblett, class 46-C recalls, "I didn't go into Tuskegee much; I didn't feel like I would be welcome there."

Rodney Custis, a member of the first class (42-C) to graduate from Tuskegee Army Air Field, put it very simply: "I seldom went into town . . . The fellows that came down, were so keen about chasing their dream and were so distressed when they washed out . . . I consider myself lucky, very fortunate. Thank God America has moved away from the forties, fifties and sixties."

Eventually, orientation classes were started to help the blacks newly arrived at the field to understand the racial prejudice of the south. The orientation was especially needed for those who arrived from the northern parts of the country. While they suffered from prejudice in the north,

it was more subtle than in the south. John Leahr still remembers part of his orientation. He recalls the instructor saying that if you get into trouble, "the military is not going to help you, the government is not going to help you . . . you will have to suffer the consequences . . . the local police are the ones you will have to contend with. . . . You are down here to fly airplanes, not to change any customs."

Off base housing would always be a problem for the training center. The shortage was particularly severe for the civilian workers because early on there were no facilities for them on the base. Many of the local citizens went out of their way to rent rooms even though there was no financial need to do so. Eventually, two housing projects were completed on the field, but not before 1943 and 1944. Additionally, a small housing project was built in the Greenwood section of Tuskegee Institute, another near Greenforks, just outside of the town of Tuskegee. One of the housing projects on the field was a 30 acre 100-apartment complex designed for Army personnel and civilian workers. It sat on a hill on the north boundary of the field, and for its time was attractive and had the latest conveniences. It was named Mitchell Village to honor Lt. Paul Mitchell, the first member of the 99th Fighter Squadron killed in action. In early 1944, there were about 80 white officers stationed at the airfield, all of whom lived off the base, most either

Open for business, a view of the Post Exchange. (AIR FORCE MUSEUM)

in Tuskegee or in Auburn, Alabama, about 20 miles from the field.

Most of the personnel assigned to Tuskegee Army Air Field arrived at the base via the Western Railroad of Alabama that had a small passenger station located at Chehaw, Alabama. Chehaw was a settlement located about three miles east of the post. Dr. Julian Peasant, who would spend most of his service at Tuskegee as an administrative officer, remembers the Chehaw railroad station as a "one horse station with perhaps just one barn like room with a platform . . . Just a station there, hardly any farms around, a very lonely place." Part of the access road from Tuskegee to the base was not paved and in wet weather became "a sea of mud." The problem was not fixed until late April 1943.

Lieutenant Lawrence Hawkins, his wife Earline and oldest son Lawrence Jr., sitting near a runway at Tuskegee Army Air Field. Dr. Hawkins was in the first Celestial Navigation class at Hondo AAF. Following the war, Dr. Hawkins would spend his career in education and retired in 1987 as Senior VP at the University of Cincinnati. (HAWKINS)

By January 1943, the major construction of the post was completed. Continued improvements would be made throughout its existence to increase efficiency and improve troop morale. As an example, late in 1942 about one hundred thousand trees were planted in an attempt to solve the severe soil erosion problems. An amphitheater was built on the northern part of the post utilizing the natural contour of the land to create the seating and stage area. Here, many USO shows would perform in order to entertain the men and women stationed at the field. The amphitheater opened on May 31, 1944. Civilians and military were entertained by Ella Fitzgerald and the Inkspots. Other USO shows entertained the soldiers, one of which had Louis Armstrong playing before a crowd of over 3000 in one of the field's hangars. Other famous entertainers to appear at Tuskegee included Lena Horne, who drew large crowds with her singing and willingness to mix with the soldiers.

Eventually a movie theatre was put into operation, and a beach with a picnic area was constructed, utilizing one of the streams that flowed on the base. Evidently the "swimming pool" was just a wide spot in the creek and did not appeal to the men. For example, the July '45 base history report states the pool ". . . is forever shallow and muddy." The same report also notes "Tuskegee Army Air Field is the only station in the Eastern Flying Training Command without a gym. The need for a gym is acute; however the base never got a gym." By late 1944, the post library contained 2,125 books and the base newspaper *The Hawks Cry* was being published weekly.

By early 1943, there were 121 cadets taking flying training. Originally, the program was set for a much lower number, but negative reaction to the quota system for black pilots put pressure upon the War Department to allow more African-Americans the opportunity to fly for their country. This was one of the primary reasons for the formation of the 332nd Fighter Group. The additional pilots would be funneled into the 332nd Fighter Group after the 99th was filled.

The formation of the 332nd and the continued presence of the 99th Pursuit squadron at Tuskegee made the primary mission of the field, Basic, Advanced, and Transition training, very difficult. In addition to the administrative problems,

Top photo: A view of the interior of a derelict building at the former training field. This was probably the enlisted men's club. Bottom: One of the many roads that formerly ran through the base. Weeds and brush are slowly covering this one.

complished. At best, it was a complicated and confusing situation.

Some of the overcrowding was relieved in March 1943 when the 867 men and 50 officers of the 332nd Fighter Group were transferred to Selfridge Field in Michigan. They were followed by the 99th Fighter Squadron in April. This unit had been on alert to move since the previous August. In late 1943, the 553rd Fighter Squadron was formed at Tuskegee to absorb pilots who had completed transition training but were not immediately sent to the 332nd. Also, a few pilots were transferred to Mitchell Field, New York. By early 1944, the 553rd Fighter Squadron was located at Walterboro Army Air Field, South Carolina. The squadron served as a replacement squadron for pilots in the 99th and 332nd Fighter Squadrons that were in combat. Other changes in 1943 included the training of liaison pilots of the Field Artillery and the start up of the training of twin engine pilots.

there was the need to train these other units. This was not the responsibility of Tuskegee Army Air Field, but of the Third Air Force headquartered in Tampa, Florida. Since there were no adequate facilities for the training of the 332nd at Tuskegee, practically no tactical training was ac-

The twin engine training started in September with the AT-10 aircraft. The first twin engine class consisted of nine pilots who were then assigned to Mather Field, California for transition training in B-25s. By early 1944, the students who finished their transition training were being sent to the 477th Medium Bombardment Group at Godman Field, Fort Knox, Kentucky for tactical training. This was a newly formed group and was in the organizational stage in

TOP: **More building remains, probably what's left of a foundation for a warehouse.**

MIDDLE: **This is a photo of the interior of the former water filter station. On the back wall is an outline of the placement of electrical equipment used to run the pumps, filters, etc.**

BOTTOM: **Some chimneys may still be seen standing in the former cantonment area.**

early 1944. Towards the end of March 1945 the AT-10 used for twin engine training was replaced with the TB-25. In order to provide a more appropriate auxiliary field for take off and landing practice, the Troy Municipal Airport was used. The town is about 50 air miles south and west of Tuskegee, and for a while some personnel had to be flown to the field each day to help conduct operations. Later facilities were built at the field, and a civilian crash truck crew was hired so that only the ambulance crew was required to make the trip.

Another important change in late 1943 was that Aviation Cadets who had been eliminated from flight training were now allowed to take training as navigators and bombardiers. Prior to this, cadets failing flight training were reduced to private and assigned to units on the base. This was because blacks had only been allowed training as fighter pilots, and the failed cadets were not eligible for any other type of aircrew training. Some of the early wash outs of 1942 had returned

No hangars remain along the former ramp area.

The approximate area where the Chehaw railroad station was located. The tracks in the foreground were put in after the base closed. The main line railroad tracks are located out of the picture to the left of the old school bus.

to civilian life. During 1943, 224 pilots graduated, of which 25 were twin engine pilots.

In October, 30 men who had failed flight training were sent to Hondo Army Air Field for navigator training. They were followed in early November by 121 pilot wash outs who were sent to Keesler Field for psychological testing for bombardier training. Despite the fact that the men had previously passed psychological testing at Tuskegee, only nine were accepted at Kessler Field for Bombardier-Navigator training. The rest were returned to Tuskegee. Many on the base felt that the majority of these men were rejected at Keesler Field because of their race.

By the end of 1943, there were approximately 700 full time civilian employees working on the base. The base had 293 students, 303 officers and 1,890 enlisted men.

Liaison training started on August 2, 1943 at Griel Auxiliary Field with the arrival of 21 students. Eventually, there would be three training classes that graduated 51 pilots. The training field was about six miles from the base, and required a twice daily 12 mile round trip over dirt roads for the instructors, students, mechanics, tools, and other equipment.

Charles Dunn was in the first class of liaison pilots and is still able to recall his first flight. The first time he flew a plane was at Tuskegee. Of his first solo he remembers "as nothing more than telling me you were going to walk down to the corner." He recalls the instructors were excellent and the school was "pretty well run." There was no instrument training. Charles also remembers being grounded for a brief period because he violated rules by flying under a bridge that spanned the Tallapoosa River. His wife, Precious Riley, for a short time was a typist on the base. After learning that some of the material she typed was confidential, Precious Riley quit, fearing that she would be blamed if the information were found out.

With our victory in Europe and the Pacific, training slowed, but pilot training continued at the field. Since there was no place to send them, they stayed on the base. By the end of October 1945, there were 106 officers and flight officers awaiting further assignment. At this point, the base had a total personnel strength of 2,536 men and women either assigned or attached. The last class to graduate was 46-C in June 1946. The class resembled the early ones with just nine graduates, seven of which graduated Single Engine School, and two the Advanced Twin Engine School. In August, Col. Parrish was reassigned to Maxwell Field, and the command of Tuskegee Army Air Field passed to Lt. Col. McPherson. Lt. Col. McPherson was an old hand at Tuskegee, having served there since October 1941. His previous responsibilities at Tuskegee included Director of Basic Training, Director of Training, and his last position prior to assuming command was Deputy Commanding Officer.

On June 30, 1946 the field was inactivated. During the training field's existence it graduated a total of 992 pilots. This included 673 from the Single Engine school, 252 Twin Engine graduates, 51 Liaison pilots, 11 Service Pilots, and 5 Foreign Pilots (Haitians).

Following the war, the field reverted back to the town of Tuskegee. Many of the buildings were moved into the town, and some saw service as part of a hospital, others served as living quarters, etc. Two of the hangars were moved, one to Montgomery, Alabama, and the other to Clanton, Alabama. In 1976, an attempt was made to develop the land as an oil refinery, but this did not work out and eventually a private owner purchased the land.

A photo of John Leahr taken at Tuskegee AAF in 1946. As a member of the 332nd Fighter Group, John flew 132 combat missions in the P-39, P-47, and P-51. (LEAHR)

The accomplishments of the black airmen trained at Tuskegee are legendary and best summed up in the pamphlet, *The Tuskegee Airmen Story (A speech guide)* prepared by the East Coast Chapter of the Tuskegee Airmen, Inc: "During the course of the war, the Tuskegee Airmen lost 66 pilots, killed in the combat zone, and in addition, 32 were shot down and became prisoners of war. They destroyed or damaged 409 German aircraft, over 950 units of ground transportation, and sank a destroyer with machine gun alone, which was a unique accomplishment. However, their most distinctive achievement was that not one friendly bomber was lost to enemy aircraft attacks during 200 combat missions. This success was unique because no other fighter unit with nearly as many missions could make the same claim."

A waist gunner in training. The student is demonstrating his ability to correct a malfunction in the 50-cal. machine gun while wearing a blindfold and heavy flying clothing. Note the gloves.

2

From Gunnery Training to Aircraft Storage

Kingman Army Air Field

"U.S. Army Pilot Training School Near Kingman Is Considered Possibility" announced a March 1941 article in the *Mohave County Miner*. This news seemed to confirm the hopes of many of the local residents that a training base would soon be built near the town of Kingman, Arizona. The announcement was welcome, but a bit premature because it would be a year before construction on the new training field would begin.

Even so, it was good economic news for most of the people in the then small town of Kingman, whose 1940 population was about 3,000. The city located in the north west corner of Arizona about 85 air miles from Las Vegas, was an ideal site for an air base. The flying weather was excellent and the area was sparsely populated with much of the land used for cattle and horse raising. The huge training complex would be located about ten miles north east of the town in the Hualpai Valley near a Santa Fe railroad siding named Berry. The primary purpose for the new training field was to train aerial gunners for the B-17. Additionally, the field trained hundreds of B-17 co-pilots, and after the war was a temporary storage site for the sale and scrapping of thousands of military aircraft.

All of this was in the future when Major John Horton arrived at the site in March 1941 to check out the suitability of the area for a new training field. The major met with various local officials to look at transportation facilities, land ownership, the possibility of electric service to the base, and the water supply. One thing was certain; the proposed site was remote. In fact, one resident described it as being like the outback of Australia.

Dick Schneider took gunnery training here and then went on to fly 28 missions with the 381st Bomb Group. He arrived in the fall of 1943 and recalls thinking, "I was just out in the desert, isolated, and far from the town of Kingman."

Before any significant construction could begin, leases had to be signed and the land had to be surveyed. At least one lease was signed in April 1941, and surveyors were at work in June of the same year, but the site was not officially approved until May 1942. The delay in site approval may have been because there was a concern about the water supply, or the fact that other sites had a higher priority. Once approval was obtained, some key base personnel moved into temporary quarters at the Harvey House in downtown Kingman, and at that point construction began. Kingman Army Air Field would require more space than most Air Forces training

An aerial view of Kingman Army Air Field as it appeared in April 1943. At this point training was in progress with the field still under construction. (MOHAVE MUSEUM OF HISTORY & ARTS)

Kingman airfield as it was circa 1995. At the top of the photo and at the base of the mountain range were located the ground to ground ranges. Several of the former ranges still exist today.

Kingman. This was called the Yucca Sub-Base, and was spread out over 583,865 acres; most of the land was devoted to firing ranges.

To obtain land for a new base, the War Department would lease or purchase the land from individuals. Sometimes a municipality held the land in hopes of the military building a base near their town. In any case, landowners were given short notice with little chance of appeal to move off the land and to accept the price offered by the government. In general, the government tried to be fair in its dealings, but it was almost always a shock and a hardship to be forced off your land with little notice. The price of the land could be contested in court and often was, but the landowner normally was forced to move. One of the landowners affected by the building of the new field was John M. Neal who raised cattle and horses on a large section of the soon to be base. John's granddaughter, Lenore Hafley, recalls that the government notified her grandfather of the pending training base and told him "they were going to use the land for target ranges and he had to move off the land or suffer the consequences. They also intended to construct some buildings on the land." He was given the choice to stay or leave. If he stayed, there was the possibility that he would lose some of his cattle due to accidental shootings. Her grandfather thought it over for about three days and decided to remain on the land. Even though most

fields because its primary mission was to train gunners. This required firing ranges that covered huge tracts of ground for the three types of gunnery training ranges. The ranges were ground to ground, air to ground, and air to air. As an example, one set of ranges was located near the town of Yucca about twenty miles from

A partial view of the ramp as it is today. Note the many concrete slabs in the former cantonment area that mark the locations of buildings since torn down.

of the land was used for target ranges, only 12 head of cattle were lost to shootings. After the war, the land was returned to her family along with the buildings constructed by the government. The buildings were a "tremendous blessing" to the family and some of the buildings are still in use today.

Because of the overwhelming need for aerial gunners during World War II, seven flexible gunnery schools were constructed. Kingman Army Air Field was the sixth built for this purpose. The others were Las Vegas Army Air Field (the first), Harlingen Army Air Field, Texas, Tyndall Field, Florida, Buckingham Field, Florida, Laredo Army Air Field, Texas, and Yuma Army Air Field, Arizona. Since Kingman was one of the last, it profited from the experience of those that had preceded it. Much of the training at Kingman would be patterned after the already operating Las Vegas Gunnery School (today's Nellis Air Force Base). The Las Vegas Gunnery School would be called upon frequently during

the startup of Kingman for personnel, equipment, and advice.

Construction of the new base started in June 1942 with the building of a boundary fence. By the third of August, construction of the three runways (the longest 6500') had started. The intent was to build the base as quickly as possible, and as a result, thousands of construction workers and military personnel descended upon the town. This unprecedented influx of people put an incredible strain upon the town's available facilities, mostly housing. Since there was not enough living space, many construction workers and military personnel lived in tents, trailers, shacks, and other structures not intended for living quarters. Complicating matters was the construction of the nearby Davis Dam. To ease the situation, work on the dam was halted at the end of December 1942. This helped the overcrowding somewhat, but adequate housing remained a critical problem. Meanwhile, the population of the base grew rapidly. The estimated

ABOVE: Two of the field's original control towers. The one on the left is of wood and was later replaced by the one on the right, 1943. This replacement tower still exists today. (USAF)

AT RIGHT: The WW II control tower as it appears today. No longer in use it is in excellent condition.

number of military on the base at the end of October was 24 men, but by the end of December this had grown to 1,235.

Building construction was typical for the new bases of the day. Most were wood frame structures, and in the case of Kingman, painted a cream color. They were hot and dusty in the summer, and bitterly cold in the winter. Despite the heat that could go to 135 degrees in the summer, few buildings enjoyed the benefit of air conditioning. John Hoza remembers arriving here at night at a train siding just outside the field, and then marching to the field. He would take gunnery training here and be held over as an instructor in the top turret. That was in early 1944. To John the base was isolated, dry, and nothing but dirt with no grass. His recalls that his first impression was not good.

Early living conditions on the base were primitive. As an example, the medical department personnel who first arrived in September 1942 while the base was under construction, found that it was cold, it was wet, and the town was a terrible letdown from Santa Ana. The base was nowhere completed, and the quarters, to say the least, were temporary." Sanitation was a problem because of the lack of water and the

yet to be completed plumbing. There were outdoor latrines and inadequate bathing facilities. Water was heated every day at 3:30 P.M. and men who wished to bathe were required to do so between the hours of 4:30 and 5:30 P.M. The men considered themselves lucky if they could shower once per week. Also, there were no recreational facilities, and for a time the gymnasium at Kingman High School was used for basketball and badminton. Eventually, the base hospital was completed and performed its first operation on December 7, 1942 with the removal of an ingrown toenail.

The training field was built so that it had an almost identical arrangement on both sides of the centrally located parade ground. That way one half of the students could be instructed on only one half of the base. Also convenient to the living quarters on the base was the ground to ground range. This huge firing range was directly across from the base and was separated from it by a major highway (U.S. Route 66) and a busy railroad line. It was very convenient because it took only about ten minutes to truck the students from their living and instructional area to the range.

Kingman's first commander was Lt. Col. Harvey Huglin who had been involved with the construction of the field since early 1942. Col. George Henry succeeded him in late December when Lt. Col. Huglin assumed the duties of Director of Training.

The four Flexible Gunnery Training Squadrons, the 1120th, 1121st, 1122nd, and the 1123rd, were activated at the Las Vegas Gunnery School, and in late December 1942 arrived at Kingman. Training would start in January 1943. One week after training started, Kingman was designated as a B-17 gunnery school. This specialization greatly simplified the school's mission and was the result of lessons learned combined with the desperate need for B-17 gunners. The B-17 was the bomber that was carrying the brunt of the air war over Europe for the 8th Air Force stationed in England.

The building of the cantonment area (barracks, hangars, warehouses, work shops, school buildings, mess halls, a hospital, etc.) was just a step toward ensuring the field would complete its training mission. Simultaneously with the construction of the buildings, huge and complex firing range facilities had to be constructed. The size and complexity of the structures ran from the smallest sentry box to huge hangars to state of the art air-conditioned Waller Trainer Buildings. Additionally, the field had a large sub-base at Yucca, Arizona, about twenty miles south of Kingman. During 1943, thirty-two buildings were constructed here, including a 476-man mess hall and eventually two 6,000' runways. To help relieve the stupefying heat of the summer, five swimming pools were constructed. In total, the complex would have approximately 555 buildings along with several emergency landing fields.

Aircraft would be an important part of the training program; the first plane, a North American AT-6, flew into the field in late December 1942. The AT-6 "Texan" was a single engine two place advanced trainer. At first, the AT-6s had to land at the Kingman Municipal airport for servicing and gas before preceding the short distance to the training field. At the time, there were no servicing facilities on the base, and because the runways were not completed, the aircraft landed on the parking apron. The number of planes on the field grew rapidly, and by March 1944, there were 147 aircraft including 70 B-17s parked on the ramps at Kingman. Aerial traffic grew with the number of planes assigned to the field. Two tower controllers operating from a truck parked along side the runway that was in use handled early operations. As traffic increased, a wooden tower was built. Later, a much larger and taller metal tower followed this. During the first full year of operation in 1943, the field handled about 100,000-radio contacts with approaching and departing airplanes. Today, the

One of the original hangars still standing and in use today.

This hangar may have been part of the sub-depot complex.

ABOVE: This building was the base laundry. It is now in the process of being improved to house the Kingman Army Airfield Historical Society & Museum.

AT RIGHT: Norm Berge, President of the Kingman Army Airfield Historical Society & Museum, standing among some remains of the former ground to ground range.

metal tower is still at the site of the former air-field. No longer in use but in excellent condition, it remains a proud reminder of the field's former service.

The smooth operation of the training program at Kingman did not happen overnight. Many months and hundreds of changes, large and small, were required after training started to produce a well-trained gunner. There were those who said the gunnery programs were not effective until the advent of the use of live ammunition against fighter aircraft. This training improvement would not happen until early 1945, and then in limited use and only at some gunnery training bases.

Perhaps the gunnery training in World War II is best summed up by authors W. F. Craven and J. L. Cate in their study *The Army Air Forces in World War II, Vol. VI, Men and Planes*. They note: "The difficulties in flexible gunnery training were greater than those for any other flying specialty. As in the navigation program, the Air Corps had virtually no background of experience in this type of instruction. Equipment shortages were extreme, and the problem of procuring qualified instructors unusually serious. Finally, it was several years before an adequate sighting and firing system was evolved, and a practicable means of simulating actual combat firing was not developed before the end of the war. As a result, the performance of flexible gunners in battles was not so efficient as desired,

and the training program was a subject for continued criticism and controversy."

The gunnery training at Kingman Army Air Field began on January 18, 1943 with Class 43-8, made up of forty students. Seventeen of the students were enlisted men with armament training and the remainder were Bombardier Officers. The huge building program required to construct the facilities had preceded all this. In addition to the actual construction of the living area and the firing ranges there were other critical needs to be filled. These needs included qualified instructors, training manuals and training aids such as machine guns, turrets, and specific sighting devices. This material was sent to Kingman along with a mountain of other material needed to keep the base functioning. This included hundreds of aircraft and the repair parts necessary to keep them in the air. Additionally, the complex nature of the program required two different types of purpose built structures to handle the then state of the art Jam Handy and Waller gunnery trainers. This complex equipment required the buildings be air-conditioned, a luxury in 1943, especially on a military base.

To keep all of this functioning, there were behind the scenes thousands of support personnel who filled the mundane jobs of cooks, bakers, medical personnel, mechanics, pay roll accountants, truck drivers, typists, building maintenance men, ammo handlers, etc. In short, this huge group of dedicated people was vital to the success of the training mission.

August 10, 1943, seven months after training started. Although turret firing had been given all students, the early classes received their turret training in turrets not used on B-17s.

The curriculum for the first few classes was a five-week program. This included class room instruction and range firing. Compared to the course of instruction given later in the war, the initial course of instruction was very basic. By June 1943 the course had been expanded to seven weeks, and would be continually changed and upgraded throughout the war. This reflected the fact that training gunners was a complex business. It required state of the art training devices, combined with the realism of firing weapons from high flying aircraft at moving targets.

Here's a simplified look at the gunnery training program at Kingman as it was around mid 1943. The first week was set aside for orientation lectures given to the newly arrived students.

The school was built to train 320 students in each class; however, as in the other training bases when they started, the early classes were much smaller. This allowed for the completion of facilities, training of school personnel, and obtaining the necessary training equipment. Much of the needed material was not available when the school started training. Because of the lack of adequate equipment, the first few classes were kept at forty students. Also, because of the scarcity of ground range facilities, and a serious lack of equipment, the first class was held over one week and graduated on February 27, 1943. The first full class of 320 students (Class 43-21), did not start training until April 19, 1943.

Kingman's mission was simplified because it had been designated a B-17 gunner's school to specialize in training gunners in the use of equipment such as the Sperry Upper Local and Lower Ball turrets found on that plane. Even so, there was a significant equipment shortage in the first few weeks of the school's existence. This included the lack of any target tow planes. The first did not arrive until the end of January and was used for the training of two pilots. Other scarce items included shotgun shells, teaching materials, and instructors. At first, instructors came from the Las Vegas Gunnery School, and Kingman students who graduated and were held over as instructors. Even though the field was a B-17 gunner's school, the first B-17 was not used for air firing until

A typical sign designating a ground range, 1943. (USAF)

An interior view of the Waller Trainer with the operator in the upper center at the console. (USAF)

Along with orientation, the students received instruction in the use of high altitude flying equipment, a high altitude pressure chamber test, military drill, military courtesy, first aid classes, and chemical warfare instruction.

In the second and third week, classroom instruction began in subjects such as weapons, turret maintenance, aircraft recognition (27 different types) and sighting. During this time, the student was introduced to the Jam Handy trainer. First utilized by the Navy and called the 3A-2, the Jam Handy utilized motion picture technology to project actual combat situations on a movie screen with sound effects that included engine noise. The attacking aircraft could be shown coming from different angles at the trainee who stood behind a non-firing machine gun. His skill in selecting the proper point of aim could be measured. Another sophisticated training device was the Waller Trainer. Similar, but more complex and realistic than the Jam Handy, it was not ready for student use until September 1943. Late in the year, instruction in the Waller Trainer was stopped because the training film was not considered current. Late in 1944, new film arrived and all eight trainers were put back into operation. Since the temperature at Kingman could reach 135 degrees in the summer, the air-conditioned buildings required by

the Jam Handy and Waller trainers were a blessing for the students and their instructors.

During this time the student also fired BB guns at the BB Range, and the .22 cal. rifle (both later eliminated), and did turret practice. He also fired shotguns on one of the 15 skeet ranges, and improved his skill at the Moving Base Range, and the Turret Shotgun Range. The moving base range was an exercise where the student fired from a moving base (the flat bed of a truck) at a moving target, a clay pigeon. The Turret Shotgun Range was set up to fire shot guns mounted in an aircraft turret on a truck at moving clay pigeon targets. Prior to this time (about March to May), the student fired on a trap range, but this type of firing was discontinued.

More range firing at ground targets continued during the fourth week of training. All were designed to teach the students the proper elements of leading a moving target and the operation of the complex turrets. Eventually, there were five moving target ranges at Kingman. At first, each student was allocated a total of 1,130 rounds of 30 cal. and 50.cal. ammunition for practice using the hand-held and turret operated machine guns. By late August 1943, this had been increased to 2250 rounds. By early summer, the 50 cal. turret firing was discontinued.

The fifth and sixth weeks were spent firing

from aircraft and this was the final part of their training. The first of the two weeks firing was done at the main base at Kingman; the second was completed at the sub-base at Yucca, Arizona. This phase of firing utilized, among other things, high altitude firing with gun cameras, firing at towed targets, and firing at ground targets.

The students also practiced firing at ground targets while flying in the B-17. John Hoza, who by then was an instructor in the upper turret, enjoyed the air to ground strafing. He recalls that "I would ride with the other instructors to help with the students. Once in a while a stray steer would wander onto the range and take relief from the sun in the shade of a target shack. The ranchers did not seem to worry much about this because they didn't think the students could hit the target shack."

To give the ranges a more personal touch, several were given names such as "Smakajap Range," "Hun Hunter Range," "Bugs Bunny's SNAFU," "Zero Buster" and "Bop-A-Wop." The Malfunction Range, not wanting to be outdone, was named "Gremlin Sanctuary."

Dick Schneider, who took his training here in the fall of 1943, remembers that "the training was quite rigorous; I was amazed at what I learned and what I had to learn. They taught a lot of theory . . . I was trained for all positions including waist gunner. I remember getting into the ball turret but was too tall for it, so they had to force me into it in order to close the hatch. I made two revolutions in it, and that was enough. I got out . . . I never had a pass while in training and I graduated with high marks. They wanted me to stay on as an instructor, but I said no, because I wanted to get into combat." Of his 28 combat missions 27 were flown as a tail gunner.

Late in 1943, the B-17 was introduced into training at Kingman, and with this started the high altitude gun camera missions, and the firing at ground targets. Firing at ground targets started in late December. At first it was very informal. The gunner would shoot at bushes and other targets while the plane flew at low level.

As a child, Lenore Hafley remembers the big red squares that were laid out on her father's ranch and were used as targets. She recalls they

A partial view of the field while still under construction. Note the large building and the unpaved roads. (USAF)

Opening of the PX. The furnishings are rather Spartan and over time will be improved. (USAF)

were made out of cloth (a silk-like material) and she would watch the planes fly over and shoot at them. She remembers that lots of women would cut pieces from the targets and used them to make dresses. There was also some air to ground firing at a dry lakebed near her home. Often it would frighten her, and when it started she would run into her home and hide under something.

Toward the end of December 1943, a number of Chinese Officers arrived at Kingman for gunnery instruction. This presented quite a problem for the training department to teach gunnery to men who did not understand English. One of the printers was particularly challenged with the order to print a 25-page booklet about the machine gun—in Chinese.

Commenting upon the progress of Kingman Army Air Field during 1943, the base history notes that "1943 was a year of steady growth

This photo of Dick Schneider was taken at Ridgewell, England (Station 167) when he was nearing the end of his tour. Dick flew a total of 28 missions, 26 as a B-17 tail gunner over Europe.

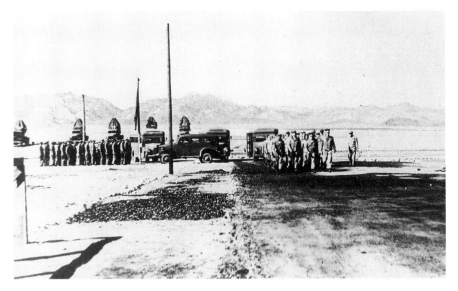

In this photo it appears that the students are returning from the machine gun range following a training session. (KINGMAN AAF HISTORICAL SOCIETY)

and development . . . full efficiency had not been reached even by December." Even so, there were 8,131 men assigned to the field by year's end, and the new training center had graduated 10,861 students. The school that started out with the name, Army Air Forces Flexible Gunnery School, Kingman, Arizona was renamed Kingman Army Air Field in May 1943.

The base had its own newspaper, *The Cactus,* published in the town of Kingman by the local American Legion Post. The first issue came out on March 2, 1943. Later on, the paper was published on the base because of government regulations that stipulated that no advertising be allowed in an "official" base newspaper. The first issue of *The Cactus* announced that Bugs Bunny was appointed the official mascot. The character was chosen because of the numerous rabbits that lived in and around the site of the post. Another newspaper, a departmental one, called *Turrettalk* was published by the instructors. It included information on teaching methods, equipment, and the latest in training aids.

The year 1944 opened with a tragic note for the men and women of Kingman Army Air Field. There were two major accidents that cost the lives of 39 men stationed on the field. The first accident occurred on January 2, and involved a B-17 that was returning to Kingman in poor weather. The aircraft broke up in mid-air, and crashed killing 13 Army men, 11 of whom were assigned to Kingman Army Air Field. The only sur-

vivor was Major James Wergen who returned to duty after about four months in the hospital.

The second accident involved the railroad tracks that separated the base living area from the ground to ground firing ranges and ran directly in front of the main entrance to the base. This was a busy set of tracks, with about forty trains per day, ranging in speeds varying from fifty to ninety miles per hour. There were large numbers of students and hundreds of civilian workers and service men living in the town of Kingman who crossed the tracks daily. A request to build an underpass for the railroad had been made but the request was not acted upon quickly.

On the night of January 6, 1944 twenty-six aviation cadets, their gunnery instructor, and the bus driver who were returning from a night gunnery class were killed when a fright train struck the bus. The death toll was the worst in Arizona history. Following this tragedy, the needed underpass was built.

By early 1944, the influx of students to the new gunnery base had increased dramatically compared to the previous year. As an example, during the January to April time frame, the number of new students averaged between 370 to 575 per week. Reflecting this increased pace of training, the expenditure of ammunition during March and April was about 17 million rounds.

The training program during 1944 was continually upgraded and changed where necessary to improve the quality of the gunners graduating from the field. Some topics were added and others dropped and, where appropriate, more time was spent on certain subjects. For example to help improve instruction, an instructor's school was

An aerial view of the still remaining triangular shaped ranges for the ground to ground firing range.

the first class to take the six-week course remembers that the orientation flight took place in the 5th week. He recalls that "about half the men had never been in an airplane in flight before and about half threw up during the flight."

Another change in the program was that weapons instruction was increased. Now the student would be required to disassemble, assemble, and adjust his machine gun while wearing winter flying gloves. The use of cold weather flying gear was a result of lessons learned from combat where the majority of B-17 missions were flown in the extreme cold encountered at high altitude. The use of the B-17 as a gunnery trainer had started in mid 1943. This change helped to improve the realism of the training especially as it related to the use of machine guns at extreme altitudes.

Range facilities were improved with better equipment and the latest sighting instruments. For a short time, liaison aircraft (Piper Cub types) were used to help the students learn proper tracking procedures and target framing during simulated attacks. By this time the field was using several different types of aircraft to fulfill its training mission. These included the AT-6, B-17, B-26, P-39, and the P-63. Toward the end of September, all the AT-6s were transferred from the field and replaced by the BT-13.

Along with the improvements in procedures and the training facilities, many steps were taken to enhance the recreational opportunities of the field. One of the more popular changes was the establishment of a rest camp about a half-mile from the rim of the Grand Canyon. The facility was a former Civilian Conservation Corps camp, located near the then well known EL Tovar Hotel. About 50 enlisted men and officers from the field visited the camp each week to participate in activities such as mule trips into the bottom of the canyon, baseball, football, tennis, hiking and horseback riding.

started to train graduate students in teaching methods prior to their being assigned as aerial gunnery instructors. One of the key simulator trainers, the Jam Handy, was upgraded as was the Waller Trainer. The student gunner pre-flight course was expanded to help the students better handle their first exposure to air to air firing. It was probably during 1944 that orientation flights were flown by each student upon his arrival at the school and before starting the gunnery course. This was a significant improvement because most students had never flown in an aircraft prior to being assigned to gunner's school, and many had expressed a fear of flying. John Hoza who was in

These structures still remain in the area of the ground to ground ranges. They may have been part of the clay pigeon target-firing complex.

Kingman Army Air Field was now a Co-Pilot Transition School. So on January 24, the first class of 110 officers began their course of instruction.

The school started with six pilot officers as instructors and no prescribed curriculum for the academic training of the students. Since no enlisted men had been assigned to the school, the officer instructors had to handle the clerical and utility work in addition to their normal responsibilities. At first, the flying training of the students was slipshod because of the lack of any precedent and the attitude of the first pilots; most had no enthusiasm for the job, because they did not want to become instructors.

By the end of 1944, The Four-Engine Transition Group had become better organized. There were improved facilities, effective training aids, and well thought out lesson plans. About 190 officers were graduated every five weeks.

Another new program that started in August 1944 was a B-26 co-pilot training school for the WASP (Women Airforce Service Pilots). This was a two-week program with about eight hours of B-26 time and 20 missions attacking B-17 formations. They would also fly the Marauders in target towing missions. The program was short lived as it only lasted until October 1944 when the B-26 training at Kingman ended. During this brief period of time, there were 20 WASPs stationed at the base.

By the end of 1944, the training of gunners had moved from the "learn from experience-local initiative stage" to a school that saw much more involvement and direction from higher headquarters. The base history states this evolution well: "There was no deviation from the trend towards standardization of gunnery schools. Flexible gunnery training became more and more inflexible." The year 1944 was the only full year of gunnery training at Kingman Army Air Field. The numbers are impressive. During the year, the school graduated 20,438 gunners, and consumed approximately 87,350,000 rounds of 30-cal., 50-cal. and shotgun ammunition. Of all the students who entered the course, 1,561 were eliminated, 230 of those for fear of flying. There were 27 student fatalities.

A new program that started in late January 1944, was a Co-Pilot Transition School. Actually it came as quite a surprise to the field when 75 pilots announced their presence at base headquarters. No one at headquarters quite knew why the officers had been assigned to the field. A check with the higher headquarters revealed that

Following the war, Kingman AAF was used as temporary storage depot and later as a scrapping facility for USAAF aircraft. Here are seen many P-38s awaiting their appointment with the smelter. (KINGMAN AAF HISTORICAL SOCIETY)

This building is one of several still existing at the ground to ground range.
It was probably used for vehicle maintenance.

A classic photo of hundreds of veteran B-17s sitting in the sun at Kingman prior to being either sold or scrapped. These aircraft were flown into Kingman from their former bases. Note the many different combat groups shown in this photo. (KINGMAN AAF HISTORICAL SOCIETY)

Kingman AAF was the scrapping location for many types of aircraft. Here are seen P-47s with some parts removed. The next step was probably stripping of their powerful engines. (KINGMAN AAF HISTORICAL SOCIETY)

By early 1945, the air war over Europe was noticeably improved especially as it related to the loss of B-17s due to enemy fighter attack. This in turn reduced the need for replacement gunners, and as a result, they soon began to stack up at the training center. At the end of February, there were 2300 graduates of the school held over at the training center. To help solve the problem a temporary tent city was built at the sub-base at Yucca to house the men. These were not happy campers. They were fully trained gunners, many of whom were looking forward to putting their skills to use. They were now stuck in the middle of the desert with very limited recreational facilities and little to occupy their time. To help morale, a furlough program was started and three day passes were given out more freely than in the past.

Meanwhile, improvements in the training process continued even as the need for replacement gunners was slowing dramatically. One of the major improvements in gunnery training was the introduction of a special bullet that could be fired at a modified aircraft without causing damage. The aircraft was called the RP-63 (a modified Bell P-63 Kingcobra), which first arrived at the training center in February 1945. The aircraft was nicknamed "The Pinball." The bullet was a 30-cal. shell designed to be fired by specially modified machine guns and would, upon impact with the target aircraft, disintegrate. It was the ideal training tool to teach gunners air to air firing against an attacking fighter aircraft. There were problems with some shells causing damage to the attacking aircraft and adapting the machine guns to fire the rounds. There were instances where gunnery students using the new frangible bullet shot down the P-63s. This didn't happen at Kingman because the program never really got started. These problems and the general slow down of gunnery training at Kingman after April 1945 resulted in few gunners being trained using the new system.

During April there were two major changes at the training center. First, the base received word in April that no more classes would be trained in the B-17 Flexible Gunnery Training Program. The graduate gunners would be screened for a B-29 gunnery program. The other major change was the cancellation of the Four-Engine Co-Pilot Transition Program.

The shut down of the base began in June 1945 when on the 8th; the public relations officer received word that the base would be tem-

Part of the smelter operation at Kingman after the end of the war. Here two workmen are pouring molten aluminum into a container.
(KINGMAN AAF HISTORICAL SOCIETY)

Kingman Air Field is still in the business of converting some aircraft and scrapping others. Here are two Lockheed 1011s with engines removed sitting in the sun.

porarily inactivated as of June 30. One of the first steps toward shutting down the base was to transfer some of the enlisted men to other posts, while others were shipped to separation centers, and still others sent to B-29 training. Students (most of these were probably the held over graduates) were sent to other bases such as Laredo Army Air Field, Lowery Field, Luke Field, Douglas Field, Williams Field, and some to other posts.

The Ground School stopped classes on June 21st. As the enlisted men were transferred from the base, the barracks they lived in were consolidated from seventeen to five. A good example of the huge size of the training program is indicated by the quantity of material transferred from the base during its shutdown. This material included 6,344,026 rounds of cal. 30 ammunition, 2,003 cal. 50 machine guns, and 5,611,344 rounds of cal. 50 ammunition. The aircraft were transferred to other fields. About half were gone by mid-June and the remainder by the end of the month. During its time as a training base, the school graduated 34,759 gunners. There were thirty student fatalities during

this period, and 3,056 students were eliminated from the school for various reasons.

While the field was in the process of being shutdown, plans were being made to use it for the temporary storage and scrapping of surplus military aircraft. The Reconstruction Finance Corporation ran this program. Early in October 1945, about 700 officers and enlisted men from Stinson Field, Texas were sent to the former training center to begin the process of activating what was to be called Sales Storage Depot No. 41. The new mission of the field was to receive excess military aircraft and sell the aircraft to private individuals or, when appropriate, scrap them for their parts, and turn the remainder into aluminum ingots. At this time, the field had been transferred to the Air Technical Service Command.

The first aircraft was flown into the field on October 10, 1945. At first, the field averaged about 43 planes per day. After November 1st, the planes came in larger numbers sometimes reaching 100 to 125 per day. By the end of December, there were about 4,693 planes parked all over the former air base. There were at least 14 different types including 2,205 B-24s and

A corner of the new Kingman Museum. This 1895 Upright Grand Piano once entertained soldiers at Kingman Army Air Field.

1,640 B-17s. Also included were B-25s, B-26s, and 34 B-32s. Some of the B-32s were probably fresh from the assembly lines.

The aircraft were flown into the field and parked. Then a group of men began to strip the plane of some equipment. This included any parts that were classified as "combat," "restricted" or "confidential." This would be items such as bombsights, guns, ammunition, radar equipment, and pyrotechnics, such as flares, flare guns, etc. After this was finished the plane was taxied to a storage area to await sale or eventual scrapping.

Apparently, the operation was planned to be larger than it was. For a while there were about 1,300 enlisted men and 50 officers stationed on the field to work on the project. Plans had been set for the field to receive about 15,000 aircraft; however, by the end of December the amount of men stationed at Kingman had been reduced to about 281.

While the scrapping operation of the field was in process, the deactivation program continued. The field closed in early 1946; however, the scrapping of the aircraft continued by a private company, the Wunderlich Contracting Company.

Today, the former training base is a thriving industrial center that retains its aviation heritage by serving as Kingman's airport. One of the several businesses on the field is a large repair and aircraft refurbishment facility, as well as an aircraft scrapping operation.

Much remains to remind the visitor of the field's proud past. The control tower still stands in its original location and is in excellent condition. Several hangars remain in good repair and are still in use by local aviation concerns. A former PX building now serves as the flight terminal, and restaurant. The former ground to ground gunnery range is just across the road. It's still owned by the same family that held it during WW II. There is much to see of the former ranges including the clay pigeon target ranges, other ground ranges, and several buildings. Here you can find bits and pieces of the targets and see the structures from which they were thrown. The former range is once again private property.

There is an active historical society on the field, and at the time of this writing (2003), it is moving into new quarters on the field. The society is run by Norm Berge who is most knowledgeable about the field and enthusiastic about preserving its memory. Norm is the driving force behind the move and is the president of The Kingman Army Air Field Historical Society and Museum.

3

Combat Crew Training

Dyersburg Army Air Field

On September 3, 1942 Captain Bernhard Jacobs of the Quartermaster Corps arrived at the small town of Halls, Tennessee (1940 population 1,511) and took command of a group of enlisted men who were stationed outside of the town. Three days later, he was sent on an overseas assignment.

Located in the middle of the Cotton Belt in an excellent farming region, the base was in the early stages of construction. Lieutenant Harold Hosler replaced Captain Jacobs as commander in addition to his duties as Base Quartermaster, and was the first permanently assigned officer to the new base. Major George Plott, commander of the 419th Base Headquarters Squadron, arrived in October. The construction that was underway had been preceded by many months of political activity, planning, surveys and involvement of people determined to have an army facility built near the town of Halls.

As early as February 1942, the local newspaper, the *Daily State Gazette*, reported activity that suggested interest in building an air base in the region. Local congressman Jere Cooper encouraged visits by Army officials. In the March 24 issue, the paper announced the War Department had approved a site and reported "Rapid Construction Program Likely Will Prevail in Building

The Field." The paper further noted: ". . . the plant will be completed by the first week of July this year, or ready to receive men for training by that date." This was not to be. The actual start of construction was several months in the future.

Apparently, the first reports on the suitability of the land for construction were not satisfactory, because the March 31, 1942 issue of the *Gazette* noted: "The decision to locate the basic field south of here was made after the original reports of the location were unfavorable." This may have been because of problems with the suitability of the land for construction, especially the cost to prepare the site for the building program. As a result, the War Department decided to build the training field at Walnut Ridge, Arkansas. This is noted in the history of Walnut Ridge Army Air Field when it referred to the reason for not building at Dyersburg. The history reports that "the construction of an overall field there (in Dyersburg) was not practical. Five million cubic yards of earth were too much to move." So, construction of a Basic Flight training base began soon after near the small town of Walnut Ridge in June 1942.

By April 2, the local paper was talking about the appraisal of approximately 4,000 acres of land and that the occupants of the land had been

39

Aerial view of Dyersburg Army Air Field (Arnold Field) as it appears today. The parking ramp and former cantonment area are in the center of the photograph. (TIM BIVENS VIA DELBERT NEWMAN)

Another view of the ramp and the former cantonment area. (TIM BIVENS)

unofficially told to look for another place to live. Anticipating the land would soon be taken over for the new training base, farming on the land had come to a stop. Still, there was no confirmed information about the new base other than the site had been approved. By April 13 offices to buy land for the site were opened and the Dyer building in Halls was leased for engineering office space. Some negotiations with owners had already been completed when the *Daily State Gazette* announced that work on the field would start on Thursday April 9. This was probably a bit premature because the actual start of grading did not get underway until late May. At the time, the newspaper referred to the new base as an "Operational Medium Bombardment Station."

The construction site was in Lauderdale County, and was reported to consist of 2,603 acres, most of which was prime farmland used for raising cotton. The official history of the base lists its size as 2,451.1 acres. In any case, there were about 72 families living on the site, all of whom had to move to make room for the new construction. The heartache and hardship

Dyersburg AAF around mid 1943. Training has started with construction still under way. Note the few aircraft and the lack of oil stains on the parking ramp. (TIM BIVENS)

worked upon those forced from their land can only be imagined. Some of the land was probably in the same family for generations, and while the purchase price may have been reasonable, being forced from the land with little notice was extremely difficult. Many farmers had to sell their livestock and equipment in order to comply with the order to vacate the land. As a result, the items were sold in a market flooded with similar items from other farms, and in an economy still suffering the effects of the Great Depression. To help with the sale of excess farm equipment and live stock, a Trade Day was scheduled for April 20 at Halls.

Some of the first army personnel to arrive at the construction site were a group of 12 men who arrived in August 1942. At the time, there were no facilities on the field so they lived in Halls, which was about a mile and a half from

the base. Later (October 1), they moved onto the field where they lived in temporary buildings that were former Civilian Conservation Corps barracks. These quarters were primitive, as was everything else at the site of the air base now under construction. There were no roads, no buildings of a permanent nature, and heat was provided by pot bellied stoves. There were no recreational facilities, and would not be any of significance until spring 1943. For entertainment, the men at the growing base would walk into Halls or look for a ride into Dyersburg. Later, a truck would make a nightly round trip into Dyersburg. By this time (October 1942), construction of the base was in full swing.

Tommy Simmons remembers the early days of the building of the air base as if it were yesterday. A long time owner of Simmons Men's Shop, Tommy's shop is at the same location in

41

A partial view of the ramp and flight line of Dyersburg AAF taken on V E Day 1945. The two large buildings on the end of the ramp are the machine shop and sub-depot hangar. Note also the octagon shaped buildings on the right of the photo. These were navigation training towers. (TIM BIVENS)

downtown Halls that it was in 1942 when the soldiers first came to Halls. Tommy recalls that the base made a tremendous improvement in the local economy. Workers, who were used to making $1 dollar a day before the war, now made $1 per hour. Prior to this, the only major source of revenue was cotton in the fall and strawberries in the spring. Soldiers lived in shacks or wherever they could find rooms. His mother rented rooms, and they had about ten different couples stay with them during 1942 to 1945.

The town had three drug stores, three pool halls, one movie theatre and seven barber shops. One of the pool halls was next to Tommy's store, and the songs that played all the time were "San Antonio Rose," the "Wabash Cannonball," "Smoke On The Water," and the "Star Spangled Banner." There were lots of strangers in the town, some of whom were a shock to the local citizens. The stores stayed open till midnight on Saturdays. You could hardly move on the streets

when the farmers came into town and joined with the soldiers from the base. Tommy remembers that the payroll for the field came in on the morning train. It was met by the Military Police with semiautomatic weapons and after the money was handed over, the cars sped off for

Mr. Tommy Simmons (in the middle) and two of his friends standing in the rear of his men's clothing store.

42

A view of the opposite end of the ramp taken on the same day. There are 51 B-17s in the photo on the now oil stained ramp. (TIM BIVENS)

Another view of the flight line showing the navigation training towers, parachute loft, control tower, and bomb sight storage building. The bomb sight storage building is the small building sitting parallel to the ramp, has four windows, two doors, and is to the right of the control tower. Note also the ditching pool in the right of the photo next to the road with a curve. A B-17 fuselage sits in the pool. (TIM BIVENS)

the base. At the time, Halls had just one police officer so the MPs helped patrol the town. Tommy still remembers them because they would stop in his shop from time to time for a chat. Two of the officers he called Stanley and Stein.

The first permanent commanding officer of Dyersburg Army Air Field was Major Calwert Tazwell, who would serve for just a short time until being replaced by Colonel Emile Kennedy in October 1942. Col. Kennedy was commander for about a year, during which he was responsible for the difficult and sometimes thankless task of overseeing the base construction and the beginning of the training program.

Construction continued through the fall and winter of 1942 and 1943, and by summer 1943 there

Dyersburg AAF control tower as it appeared in 1945.
(TIM BIVENS)

this point there, was a rapid change of commanding officers. On October 5, Major George Mackey assumed command replacing Col. Kennedy, who became commanding officer of Dalhart Army Air Field in Texas. Shortly thereafter, now Col. Moorman, who on October 30 was replaced by Col. Samuel Gurney, replaced Col. Mackey. This rapid change of commanding officers was probably more related to organizational improvements rather than a reflection on their performance. For example, Col. Mackey remained as Executive Officer, and Col. Moorman remained as commanding officer of the 346th Group.

It was during this period that the base was undergoing growing pains resulting from a lack of proper training facilities, poor aircraft maintenance, and a low level of personnel experience. This was typical for newly opened USAAF training bases during this time. New training bases were being built and put into operation all across the United States, and the demand for equipment to run the bases along with qualified people was insatiable. As a result, local initiative prevailed; homemade solutions were put into practice, and trainers used what was available. Unfortunately, some training was missed for lack of equipment or personnel, and the graduates of these schools often went into combat lacking part of their training. What may have been unique to Dyersburg was the low morale at this period. There was a lack of cooperation between the personnel receiving training and those who were responsible for their support. In one group were

were over 500 structures of all shapes and sizes on the base. More would come, but by this time the major construction phase was over and the new base was deeply involved in its training mission. In effect, a city had been built on what had just months before been prime cotton farmland and woods. By October 1943, there were 703 officers and 4,112 enlisted men either assigned to or involved in training at the base. At

Side view of the sub-depot, just after completion in 1942. (TIM BIVENS)

Two Dyersburg B-17 Fs on a training flight during 1943. The DY on the top of the vertical stabilizer indicates the aircraft is based at Dyersburg AAF. (TIM BIVENS)

the trainees who were at the base for a short time, and the other group was assigned permanently. Those permanently assigned had to contend with the lack of proper housing, recreational facilities, a raw unfinished base, and in their opinion, a thankless job that required long hours under poor working conditions.

At about the same time, a major organizational change was ordered for all bases throughout the training organization. It simplified training and housekeeping, and resulted in a more efficient training program under a unified command. The process started at Dyersburg in November 1943. The official name of the field became the 346th Combat Crew Training School, Army Air Field, Dyersburg, Tennessee. Morale and the quality of training slowly improved, thanks in large part to the forceful yet charming leadership of the new

base commander, Col. Gurney, and the continual upgrading of the facility.

Maintenance of the aircraft was a never-ending chore, especially keeping the older B-17 Fs in the air. Later, the problem of maintenance would ease somewhat as the newer B-17 G models arrived on the field. Claude "Hoot" Walkins washed out of cadet training because of eye problems and was assigned to Dyersburg Army Air Field as an "on the line trainee." Eventually, he became a crew chief on a B-17 and would serve at the base from February 1944 until August 1945 working as a mechanic. He recalls: "We had F and G models, and put in a tremendous amount of hours working six days a week alternating days and nights. The B-17 was a great old bird. The planes got a lot of rough usage." Once, after a trainee pilot had landed his plane,

A partial view of the Compass Rose as it exists today. Formerly on the base ramp, it became part of a factory floor when a building was constructed on top of it.

A small building near the flight line which was probably used to store aircraft paint, and other flammable supplies.

Walkins asked the pilot "how's the old bird flying?" The pilot replied "OK," at which time Hoot looked up and saw three push rods extending from an engine. Hoot thinks the push rod housing must have come loose soon before the plane landed. The pilot never noticed it. Hoot spent his entire time on the base without getting a promotion, finally being promoted to Private First Class just as he left the base in August 1945. The reason for the lack of promotions was that there were lots of combat returnees working on the base who had rank. This meant that there were few promotion slots available at the base for the men who had not been overseas where promotions were given more freely. This lack of promotions always had a great impact upon morale.

Housing, especially quarters for the civilian workers, remained a problem. To help alleviate the situation, a civilian housing project called Rutherford Terrace was built and put into operation in October on the southern part of the airfield. There were 134 units built of cinder block, varying from simple sleeping rooms to housekeeping apartments complete with an icebox and cooking stove. Additionally, there was a fully equipped cafeteria that served daily meals. Of interest is the correspondence between base commander, Col. Kennedy, and the National Housing Agency. Col. Kennedy was seeking advice on the naming of the project and was advised that "no names of living persons shall be used. Names with local historical or geographic significance are preferred . . ." So Rutherford Terrace was named to honor Captain Henry Rutherford who made the original survey of the part of Tennessee that held the air base. Additionally, Captain Rutherford along with members of his family is buried about four miles east of the site of the housing project. The project was officially opened on October 18, 1943.

Many of the enlisted trainees lived in buildings called hutments. The hutment was a small, one room, square shaped wooden structure, made of plywood with a sheet of tarpaper fastened over the wood to help keep out the wind and rain. To substitute for windows, there was a cutout in the wood with a sheet of plywood on hinges so that the opening could be closed to keep out inclement weather. A screen covered the opening to keep out the bugs. A pot bellied stove placed in the middle of the shack helped to keep it warm in the winter. There were no plumbing facilities in the structure, and it had room for six bunks. The barracks provided somewhat better living conditions. One of the flight engineers taking training at the time was Ken Otto. Ken remembers living in one of the old CCC (Civilian Conservation Corps) barracks that were built on stilts and were in poor condition. Ken was there only for night flight training and

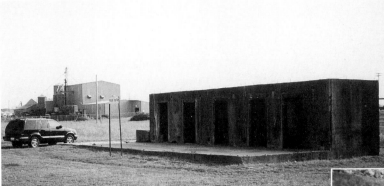

recalls: "we flew individually, taking navigation training. Once, we found ourselves somewhere over in Carolina lost and trying to figure out how to get back to Dyersburg. I mentioned to the navigator 'how about flying the beacon home?' The navigator did, and we were able to find the base." Later, Ken would fly 35 missions over Europe, and, as part of the 95th Bomb Group, was among the first to bomb Berlin.

By November 1943, much of the major construction was over and the base was adding touches that made it more livable. As an example, the hospital had added a waiting room furnished with new furniture given by the people of Ridgley, Tennessee. Flowers donated by the City Beautiful Commission of Memphis and Dyersburg graced many wards and other areas. Trees and shrubs donated by the same organization were planted. The people of Dyersburg, Halls, Ripley and Ridgley also received thanks for their part in improving the day rooms with chairs and writing desks. The base hospital was a large complex located in the southeast corner of the base, and by September 1943, had forty-five wood frame tarpaper covered buildings. These buildings housed the various departments, two operating rooms, and 350 beds for the patients, scattered among the many buildings.

Specially trained guard dogs named Duke, Scraps, Goofy, and Rascal helped maintain security on the new field. The base swimming pool now had a nine-room bathhouse, and the Enlisted Men's Service Club had been completed. The social life for the officers improved with the upgrading of the officers' club which included new furniture, a rug, game tables, and other decorations. The base newspaper, the *Vox Prop*, was by now an established feature on the base since its first edition of Friday March 5, 1943. The name was a combination of two words; one Latin meaning voice and the other English, the prop. The paper printed local base news as well as national and international military news articles on a weekly basis. One article reported on the first formal military wedding on the base between Lt. Norman Hobart, Jr. and Miss Anita Cates of Gates, Tennessee. An article in the July 23, 1943 edition told about the new USO facility in Dyersburg in the former Ozment garage building. Prior to this, the USO was in temporary quarters on Court Square. An advertisement for the Halls Theatre listed the movie schedule for the week of March 7. *Apache Trail* would follow the movie *Friendly Enemies* with Lloyd Nolan and Donna Reed, then *Wake Island* and on "bargain day" (Saturday) a double feature—*Man from Cheyenne* and *Time to Kill*. The base also had its own movie theatre that opened in March 1943. It seated 600 soldiers and charged 15 cents admission.

By January 1944, Dyersburg Army Air Field was training two classes of 56 combat crews in the second and third phase of combat crew training. These phases of training were designed to

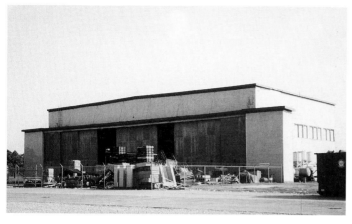

Three views of the remaining hangar at Dyersburg AAF. Today it is used for a business and is in excellent condition.

train the crew to blend their individual skills with the other crew members to function as an efficient team. In the second phase, training teamwork was stressed in the areas of bombing, gunnery, and flying the aircraft under instrument flight conditions. These training missions were flown with full crews. The next step, which was termed the third phase, also emphasized crew skills especially in the area of operating with other aircraft. During this part of the training, there were high altitude formation flights, navigation over long distances, target identification, and mock combat missions. At this time, 44 B-17s were assigned to the field.

Training, especially formation flying, was deadly business for the young inexperienced flyers. Bad weather, wake turbulence, poor timing, and reactions yet to be honed by instinct, all contributed to midair collisions and often death for the trainees, some still in their teens. Two midair collisions in January resulted in ten deaths. On one aircraft, eight crew members bailed out suc-

cessfully before the aircraft crashed near Harding, Louisiana. The other airplane, although damaged, landed safely; two died in this accident. The other midair resulted in eight deaths, about five miles from the base. Two crew members from the plane survived. During WW II in the USAAF, there were about 14,500 deaths attributed to aircraft accidents, including the death of 2,796 young men involved in 1,589 accidents with the B-17. The first fatal accident occurred at Dyersburg on May 17, 1943 when six men died in a night training crash of a B-17, one mile north of the training field. The worst single accident occurred on January 25, 1945 when 16 men were killed as a result of a midair collision. Only 10 days before this, 10 more men were killed in the crash of a B-17 in a wooded area about eight miles from the field.

One of the more sophisticated ground training devices used at Dyersburg was the Celestial Navigation Tower. This device, invented by Edwin Link, simulated flying conditions in any weather day or night using instruments, radio and the stars.

These trainers were quite advanced for their day and were contained in an air-conditioned octagonal building several stories high. In addition to the overhead display of a rotating dome

A partial view of the ramp. Square objects in background are bales of cotton in temporary storage waiting for shipment.

of stars to guide the navigators, there was a screen below the trainees Plexiglas floor on which was projected movement over the ground. The stars displayed could be adjusted to the latitude and longitude of the flight being made and the ground display would indicate the terrain using actual photographs flying over both friendly and enemy territory. To make the device more realistic, cloud cover could be changed, the altitude adjusted, and visibility changed as the "dawn breaks." This device could also be used to train bombardiers, pilots, and radio operators. Dyersburg Army Airfield had six of these expensive trainers, the first of which was probably in use around April 1944.

Another training device installed at Dyersburg was the "ditching pond." To help train B-17 crew members on the best method to evacuate after landing in water, a B-17 fuselage was placed in the middle of a man made-pond on the base. Then the crews were trained to evacuate the aircraft. This training was designed to save lives in the event that B-17 was forced down at sea. Harold Brown, a member of training crew #10406 who took training at Dyersburg in 1944, recalls that "My ten man crew took 18 seconds to get out, with five men exiting each side. We practiced it three or four times."

In early February, the base celebrated its first year in operation with an open house attended by the citizens of Dyersburg, Halls and surrounding communities. The festivities helped improve relations between the citizens and the military, that by now, had become a major factor in the lives of the people living around the new training center. The *State Gazette* reported in an editorial: "As result of the anniversary celebration, with the public given an opportunity to see what goes on at the base in the training and developing of fighting forces, the wall that has more or less separated the two ever since the base was opened here was removed."

A major change in the training program at Dyersburg Army Air Field took place in March 1944 when the field assumed responsibility for all three phases of combat crew training. The base was already doing second and third phase training. To this was added first phase training. This new training (for Dyersburg) was intended to give the individual crew member further training in his specialty. Subjects included night flying and instrument training for pilots, long distance navigation for navigators, bombardier practice and gunnery training. Now there would be 56 crews in training for each of the three phases that brought the total to 168 crews, or about 1,680 men in training at one time. At the end of March 1944, there were 939 officers, 4,217 enlisted men and 886 civilians working on the field. At the beginning of April, after a reorganization, the field was renamed "223rd Combat Crew Training School, Army Air Field, Dyersburg, Tennessee."

To help acclimate the combat crews soon to leave for duty in England, some streets and buildings on the field were renamed with the English names of a base in England. This process started in April 1944. Dyersburg Army Air Field was unofficially named Peterborough Airdrome after an operational air field of the same name in Northamptonshire, England.

The mural "Tribute" was painted by Corp. Ernest Berkowitz for the Dyersburg AAF Open House on June 10, 1945. The painting hung in the American Legion Post 161 for a number of years until moved to Hall's City Hall. Following refurbishment, a dedication ceremony was held in 1987 with the artist (now Ernest Berke) in attendance. Mr. Berke was awarded a plaque and the key to the city in appreciation of his work.

The weather at Dyersburg was a definite factor in the training at the base. Poor flying conditions often resulted in cancellation of flying training and the use of the bombing ranges. February 1944 was especially poor because flying was canceled 37% of the time. Additionally, in March, one of the high altitude bombing ranges was closed because it was under water due to flooding. Aggravating the problem was a lack of aircraft available for training due to maintenance problems. The aircraft situation was improving with the gradual substitution of new B-17s (the G model) for the older and worn out B-17s. Lack of suitable nearby gunnery ranges continued to hamper training. As late as April, the trainees had to fly about 600 miles to the Gulf of Mexico, near Gulfport Mississippi, to practice their air-to-air gunnery.

Living near a practice bombing range could be hazardous because of navigational errors or target misidentification by the inexperienced bombardiers. Often, the bombing ranges had a crude structure placed in the center of the range to indicate the aim point of the target. The bom-

bardiers were graded on how close their bombs came to hitting the target. If they actually hit the target it was called a "shack." One bombing range was near the small town of Covington, Tennessee, where apparently a bombardier misidentified his target. As a result, he dropped several practice bombs on the house of Lethe Harper. One bomb actually hit her home, going through the kitchen roof and the other two bombs landed about 30 feet from her home. Luckily there were no injuries.

Wayne Ferguson, a 20-year-old first pilot in the summer or fall of 1944, was assigned a crew in Lincoln, Nebraska and then sent to Dyersburg for crew training. One incident that still stands out in his mind after almost 60 years was the occasion when his instructor pilot cut one of his engines just as he was getting ready to flair out for the landing. Wayne remembers: "I gave it full throttle, pulled up the gear, raised the flaps and stayed maybe five to ten feet off the ground. This put me below the level of the levee in the distance and I stayed at that altitude until I gained airspeed. Then I just flew over it. The worried instructor didn't

A former barracks converted into a home in the same location where it stood on Dyersburg AAF.

At right: These remains are part of a former gunnery range. Pushed into this spot when the land was cleared; these concrete structures may have been part of a turret trainer complex.

Below: This lonely chimney still stands as a reminder of the site of the base movie theatre.

a B-17 before joining Wayne's crew. After leaving Dyersburg, Wayne was assigned to the 463 Bomb Group and flew 35 combat missions.

Weather and aircraft availability were not the only problems hampering training at the base. There was the usual lack of proper training material, expe-

know if I was going to hit the levee or fly over it." Wayne doesn't recall much formation flying; maybe two or three aircraft at a time flew formations. He also remembers that his gunners never had an opportunity to fire air to air gunnery missions. His copilot came directly from flying a T-6 (a single engine advanced trainer) and had not flown

rienced personnel, and facilities that all the training bases faced throughout the war. Added to this were three key items, gas, practice bombs, and oxygen, all of which were in danger of depletion during this period. Had not special measures been taken, the lack of any one would have seriously affected training. At one point in April the field

performance fighter with a top speed of around 400 miles per hour, which was over 100 mph faster than the B-17. Their purpose at Dyersburg was to help train gunners on interceptor practice during Wing Mission formation flights. The enthusiasm for the fighter soon waned; however, when a P-63 collided with a B-17 during a mock fighter attack. The pilot of the fighter hit the nose of the bomber with his wing, killing three men. He had misjudged his speed and rate of closure and hit the nose of the plane with his wing. The bomber crashed after the eight remaining crewmen parachuted to safety.

On March 1, 1945 a major administrative change took place when the field was transferred from the Second Air Force to the Third Air Force. The numerical designation was also changed from the 223rd Army Air Force Base Unit to the 330th. This change was a reflection of the emphasis on B-29 training in the Second Air Force. For a while there was some talk that Dyersburg Army Air Field would become a B-29 training installation, but facilities did not permit such a radical change in the training mission.

With the end of the air war in Europe in sight and no need for B-17s in the Far East, there was a definite decline in the need for new bombers and crews. Flying training was changed from three, five hour periods per day, seven days a week, to two, five-hour periods per day, six days a week. About this time, the average number of B-17s assigned to the field was increased from fifty-five aircraft to about seventy-five. Also, for the first time, fighter aircraft were based on the field to help with gunnery training. At first (March 1945), about eight P-40s were here, followed in June by the P-51. By this time the war in Europe was over, and there no longer existed a need for B-17 combat crews or their planes.

The training which had been intensive in March /April was slowing down by May, and

was down to about 60,000 gallons of gasoline on hand, with a daily use of approximately 90,000 gallons. It was feared that spring flooding would affect the normal barge delivery, so emergency shipments were requested by railroad tank car. This quick thinking in anticipation of a problem insured the field had adequate amounts of fuel. On other occasions, to meet the threat of a possible oxygen shortage, it was necessary from time to time to send trucks at night from the field to the supplier, the Linde Air Products Company in Memphis, to get oxygen. The cylinders were taken straight from the production line. The oxygen was then rushed back to base in time to fill the aircraft's oxygen tanks for the next morning's high altitude flights.

A group of four Women's Airforce Service Pilots (WASP) arrived at the field in mid-October for what would be a short stay. Since the deactivation of the WASP had already been announced for December 1944, there was little impact upon the training at the air base. They flew the L-4 (a single engine Piper Cub type plane) to help the gunners practice tracking and also flew when needed as courier pilots.

Another short-term event at the field in October was the temporary assignment of the Bell P-63 Kingcobra for use in the training of the B-17 gunners. The arrival of this sleek, little fighter was met with considerable enthusiasm on the base that had become used to seeing the huge, workhorse-like B-17. The Kingcobra was a high

Mrs. Pat Higdon standing in front of The Veterans' Museum. Pat has been a school teacher, a mayor of Halls, and is the driving force behind the preservation of the proud history of Dyersburg AAF.

stopped in August. The end of the war in Europe, followed by the defeat of Japan in August brought to a close the training of bomber crews at Dyersburg Army Air Field. During the short time between the start of training (May 1943) until it stopped, more than 1,000 combat crews were trained. The cost was high; 114 young men lost their lives in training accidents.

Following the discontinuation of training in August, the field was placed on standby status. There was the normal flurry of political activity by civic leaders and politicians in an attempt to keep the field open, but it was of no use. The field would close. The shutdown represented a severe economic blow to the surrounding communities; however, the temporary nature of the buildings coupled with the poor flying weather in winter prevented any serious consideration for its continued use in the post war Air Force.

The first of the major closing activities involved the reduction of personnel assigned to the base, so that by the end of September, there was a total of just 1,621 military personnel at Dyersburg along with 740 civilian workers. This was far in excess of the official authorization issued in July that allowed for just 29 military personnel and 100 civilian workers. At the beginning of August, there were 72 B-17s at the training base, and by September only three remained. The field had grown strangely quiet.

Today there is little in the way of remaining WW II structures to remind visitors of the proud history of Dyersburg Army Air Field. One hangar, several smaller buildings, and a bank vault type structure for the storage of the Norden Bombsight is about all that's left. One runway still welcomes visitors to the field, and a close look around the field will reveal some converted buildings. A manufacturing facility has been built on the part of the ramp that contains the compass rose. Here, the radius lines for the compass rose are still visible in what is now the floor of the manufacturing facility.

Today the former training base is called Arnold Field. There is an excellent and growing museum named the Veteran's Museum located on the ramp where the B-17s once parked. It was founded by Pat Higdon, the former mayor of Halls, and a dedicated corps of volunteers including her husband Sonny and Dyersburg Army Air Field historian Tim Bivens. The museum has held yearly air shows since 1993, well attended tributes to those who served here. It's well worth your time to visit.

Trent Ferrell standing next to the DC-3 that he flies for Miami Valley Aviation. MVA is a large freight and passenger operator that flies a fleet of wonderfully maintained DC-3s, C-47s and executive aircraft out of Hook Field in Middletown, Ohio.

An aerial view of Venice Army Air Field taken in 1943. Note the Gulf of Mexico in the lower right hand corner.
(VENICE ARCHIVES AND AREA HISTORICAL COLLECTION)

The Venice Army Air Base main entrance was located at the intersection of
The Rialto and San Marco Drive. (VENICE ARCHIVES AND AREA HISTORICAL COLLECTION)

4

On the Job Training

VENICE ARMY AIR FIELD

Venice, Florida is a vibrant growing community sitting on the Gulf of Mexico, beckoning winter tourists with its warm weather and sandy beaches. Like the rest of Florida, the city's growth over the past few decades has been explosive. With an expanding population of over 19,000, the city is far removed from what it was in 1940.

Then, Venice was a sleepy small town of about 509 citizens who gained some of their income from the brief winter tourist season.

All would change in early March 1941; when the military showed interest in the area near Venice. Some of this interest came as a result of a telegram sent to the War Department by Mr. Finn Casperson of the Venice Shores Real Estate Company. Mr. Casperson was probably working in concert with the chamber of commerce defense committee, and others, including prominent local citizens. Knowing the tremendous boost to the local economy that would result from a nearby army installation, Mr. Casperson offered 3000 acres of land near Venice for use as an army campsite. The War Department reacted quickly, and in the same month sent a military detail to check out the site. The results of the survey were favorable, and a public announcement soon followed. The July 16, 1941

issue of the *Sarasota Herald Tribune* reported: "Army Picks Venice Site for Probable New Camp." The paper further reported that about 30,000 men would be stationed at the new camp, and it would likely be used as an anti-aircraft artillery installation.

Many of the people of Venice were delighted with the news of the military project, and their enthusiasm continued to build when surveys for the new camp were started in August. By January 1942, the surveys were completed and the U.S. Engineers office was closed; however, the hoped for construction, with the resulting rapid stimulus to the local economy, did not happen. In fact, over the next several months nothing was done on the project, causing many citizens to doubt that a base would be built. For reasons not clear, the land was never used for an anti-aircraft artillery site.

Later in 1942, the Air Forces became interested in developing a training center on the already surveyed site. The plan was to establish a small training facility to accommodate about 1,000 men, with the possibility of expanding the facility at a later date. The mission of this training complex was somewhat unique. Its purpose was to train organizations whose members would be proficient in airplane maintenance and

The intersection of The Rialto and San Marco Drive today.

tary Institute. The Florida Medical Center, a private hospital, was owned and operated by Dr. Fred Albee M.D., a well-known orthopedic surgeon. Dr. Albee, who owned much of the land the base would occupy, was willing to lease the land for a small sum or at no cost. Dr. Albee agreed with the military's desire to upgrade the medical center into a military hospital that would serve several training bases in the area. Over time, and with considerable difficulty, the hospital was turned into one of the more beautiful and best-equipped station hospitals of any Air Force installation of its size in the United States. The Kentucky Military Institute was near the hospital. The several buildings of the institute were considered ideal for use in the possible future expansion of the hospital.

Following a detailed look at the area, a site was selected that was on the southern limits of the City of Venice between U.S. Route 41 (the Tamiami Trail) and the city. At that time it was undeveloped land covered with pine trees, palmetto bushes, and the ever-present rattlesnakes. The site was intended to house about 900 men with the possibility of accommodating three times that number in the future. A grass air field was also located on the site, which at the time, was leased from the city to the Deane Flying School, who in turn leased it to Embry Riddle for the training of British pilots. The field was used as an auxiliary landing strip for cross-country flights and emergency landings. There was also a nine-hole golf course between the campsite and the airfield. Later, the clubhouse for the golf course would be converted into an officers club.

The City of Venice was rather small, with one movie theatre, a bowling alley, and five hotels. The large number of hotels for such a small city indicates the number of tourists (about 2,500)

supply. The trained unit would be called a Service Group, and would operate close to the front lines servicing aircraft of several combat squadrons flying from different airstrips. The group would be equipped with the tools necessary to do complex maintenance, and be mobile enough to follow the combat units. This would then relieve the combat unit of many housekeeping details, and allow the unit to focus on flying combat.

At the time, it was believed the best way to train the new Service Groups was to place a well trained and equipped "Parent Group" on a small airfield, then give the parent group the responsibility for on the job training of the trainee group. Also, the training unit needed to be located near several airfields where combat aircraft were being flown. This set-up would best approximate the simulated combat conditions necessary for good training.

With these requirements in mind, Col. Nicholson arrived at the small Venice airport in May 1942. His visit was followed by another in late May when a committee headed by Col. Nicholson took a detailed look at the potential site. In order to approve the area for a new training center many factors had to be evaluated and approved, including: transportation, the local labor supply, meteorological data, the suitability of the building area, the supply of water and power, and the availability of construction material.

Two advantages of the site (not normally found at new training center locations), were the Florida Medical Center and the Kentucky Mili-

Today's view of the former Kentucky Military Institute. The military school, located in Kentucky, had its winter quarters in Venice, Florida. Often military formations for the personnel of Venice Army Air Field were held on the school's parade ground. This photo shows part of the school's campus. The first floor had offices, and classrooms, while the second and third were devoted to sleeping quarters. Today this is the Venice Center mall that has shops on the first floor and condominiums on the second and third floors.

Former parade grounds for the Kentucky Military Institute.
(VENICE ARCHIVES AND AREA HISTORICAL COLLECTION)

for the early, rapid increase in size was that the facility (in addition to training Service Groups), would also be used as a fighter pilot training base. When completed, the new training facility would have the capacity to house over 4,000 soldiers (about 10 times the population of the city of Venice).

Over the next several months, the once overgrown and vacant land was hurriedly converted into a military installation. The training site was primitive with few amenities, but eventually would be ready to begin its task of training personnel for the Service Groups. The advance element of the 27th Service Group arrived here in early July 1942 to perform guard duty, and to help clean up the mess caused by the rapid construction. Over the next several weeks, additional personnel along with other members of the 27th Service Group arrived. By early August, the facility became officially

that stayed in the vicinity during the season.

On May 31, 1942 the Area Engineers moved into their temporary office located in the El Patio Hotel in Venice and began work. On the same day, the first truck load of tent frames arrived at the construction site. This signaled the start of construction, which began on June 7 with work on the water and sewer system. Within a short period of time three runways were being built and additional buildings were added to the original plans. What started as a relatively small installation soon grew to 1,669 acres. The reason

A street scene of Venice Army Air Field in 1942. Note the large ditches needed to carry away water from the typical Florida thunderstorm.

The base history comments on the living conditions at the time:

Life for the enlisted men at this time was very rugged. They were quartered in winterized tents and slept on canvass cots with no mattresses or pillows. This together with the policy of "no furloughs" threatened to ruin the excellent morale that had always been a pride of the 27th Service Group. However, good leadership plus a very active recreation program helped to maintain good spirit. The Gulf beaches, only a quarter mile from camp, played a big part in the recreational program.

Adding misery to the primitive living conditions was the onset of the rainy seasons that caused the inadequate sewage and drainage systems to overflow. Small ponds appeared throughout the campsite, and water was everywhere. As a result, a modern sewage disposal plant was built and the drainage ditches were improved to correct the problem.

The construction work on buildings and the grounds continued for several months to prepare the new training facility. By December 1942, when the 80th Service Group arrived for training, the camp was ready to begin its training mission. When the men arrived, they were supposed to have had their basic and technical training; however, this was not the case. Many did not have this training, and as a result, they could not go directly to their on the job training. So the school had to make considerable changes to the training curriculum that would include the necessary basic and technical instruction. To make matters more interesting, the base received a new commander; Major L.J. Callaghan replacing the just promoted Lt. Col. Hanby, who was transferred to MacDill Field.

Following the experience with the 80th Service Group, several new courses of instruction

known as the Service Group Training Center commanded by Major Frank Hanby. The 27th Service Group would be the parent group responsible for the training of new Service Groups.

At this point (early August 1942), the new training center was no where near ready to start its mission of training; construction was still in progress, and considerable work need to be completed to prepare for the arrival of the new trainees. These tasks included setting up equipment, pulling stumps, cutting weeds, building walk ways, and other housekeeping jobs (one of which was fighting mosquitoes).

P-40s lined up for maintenance at Venice Army Air Field. The picture taken around 1943 also has two P-39s across the row from the P-40s. Part of one P-39 is barely visible. Also note the Cessna UC-78 "Bobcat."
(VENICE ARCHIVES AND AREA HISTORICAL COLLECTION)

This photo shows mostly P-39s lined up on the ramp at Venice Army Air Field on June 1, 1943. Beyond the flight line and in the trees are the many hutments used by the soldiers as sleeping quarters.
(VENICE ARCHIVES AND AREA HISTORICAL COLLECTION)

After the war and in the fifties some of the buildings were converted for use as civilian businesses. They seem to have been repainted from their original drab color. (VENICE ARCHIVES AND AREA HISTORICAL COLLECTION)

were established. When new Service Groups arrived for training, the training status of the men was reviewed, and those requiring additional training were immediately assigned to the appropriate schools.

The first school set up under the new system was designed to teach the intricacies of the Allison engine, which powered Air Forces planes such as the P-40 and the P-38. Additional schools, including the Rolls-Royce engine school, a Curtiss-Wright class, and a school on the Pratt and Whitney engines followed this. Some of the other schools on the base that were non-technical included an Air Corps Supply School and an Administration School, that included a First Sergeant's school.

In addition to the technical schools in operation at the training center there were a number of basic training classes that were taught at the same time. There were classes in camouflage, aircraft identification, booby traps, field sanitation, convoys, and bivouacs. All this training and much more was necessary for the soldiers of the Service Groups who would be performing their jobs close to the action of the front lines.

By early 1943, several changes were in the wind for the Venice Service Group training base. The first of the changes was the arrival of a new commanding officer, Col. V. B. Dixon, who assumed command on February 13, 1943. At the same time, the designation of the base was changed from Service Group Training Center to Army Air Field. One of first actions of Col. Dixon was to open a base headquarters, which assumed responsibility for the operation of the base. This action allowed the 27th Service Group to focus its energies on training the men for the Service Groups. Col. Dixon also made several changes to improve the living conditions of the enlisted men. These changes included seeing that the men received better beds, mattresses, and pillows, along with establishing a system of furloughs. Prior to this the men had been sleeping on canvass cots. Also a chapel, library, theatre, and Service Club were built, all of which had a significant positive affect on the morale of the base. Later in May 1943, the 422nd Base Headquarters and Airbase Squadron arrived to operate the field. By the end of October 1943, seven Service Groups had received their training at the base.

One of the groups in training at this time was the 14th Service Group, which was made up of Chinese Americans. The group arrived on January 16, 1944, and remained at Venice Army Air Field for training until October 2, 1944. They generated considerable interest and curiosity, especially among the civilians of Venice.

Harry G. Lee was a member of the 14th Air Service Group joining the group while it was in training at Venice. Following training, the group shipped overseas, and eventually Harry would spend time in China where he would serve as

Above: While undergoing training with the 14th Air Service Group, Harry Lee and his friends would often visit the nearby beach at Venice. Here they are seen cooking hotdogs at the beach. Harry is on all fours on the extreme right of the photo. (LEE)

Right: Harry Lee and two of his friends are seen leaning against one of the rather primitive outdoor showers at Venice Army Air Field. (LEE)

assistant base engineering officer, line chief, and chief inspector. While in Chihkiang, his men worked on the P-38, P-40, P-51, B-25, C-46, and the C-47. One of Harry Lee's several awards is the Bronze Star, earned while defending his base against the advancing Japanese Army.

Before going overseas and after training at several bases, Harry was sent to Springfield, Illinois to join a new-formed group of Chinese Americans. From there they were ordered to Venice, Florida for overseas training. Harry had never heard of Venice, but reasoned it had to be better then winter in Springfield, Illinois.

Harry recalls: "While we were stationed at Venice Army Air Field, we lived in a 6 or 8 man hutment, and the weather wasn't the best. We had a few good days, but mostly the days were cold and very humid. Putting on my fatigues in the morning felt like taking them out of the bathtub and putting them on wet. In good weather, we headed for the beach. There was no real recreation area on the base; the only recreation was in the town of Sarasota."

While training in Venice, Harry took a few men in a Jeep to Orlando to get familiar with the B-25. He remembers:

... while driving through town to get to the base, I came to a crossing, and somebody in a bus yelled, "Japs! Japs!" Boy, that irritated me. I took that Jeep and swung it around, and pulled it along side the bus. I yelled "who the hell is disgracefully yelling names like that? In the first place we're in United States uniforms, we are Americans regardless of our race and creed. Second of all, we are Chinese Americans; all Asian people aren't Japanese." That bus driver just stopped that bus and would not move it until we finished chewing out the guy who made that remark. There was no racial discrimination, none whatsoever. Most of our officers were white. We had a few Chinese American Officers, but most had not been in the service long enough to make the officer grade.

The base assumed a new responsibility in June 1943 with the arrival of the 13th Fighter Squadron and later the 14th Fighter Squadron of the 53rd Fighter Group from Page Field. These units were operational training units, whose mission was to train combat fighter pilots and ground crewman. This move tied in nicely with the training of Service Groups because it added a bit of realism to the training of the Service Groups. At first, the fighter groups trained with the P-39 (this may have been at Page Field), but later switched to the P-47, then the P-40 in April 1944, and finally the P-51 Mustang. In March 1944, the sub-bases at Punta Gorda Army Air Field, and Page Field were assigned to Venice Army Air Field. What had originally been intended to be a small base for about 900 men had now grown to a base with the responsibility for more than 7000 soldiers. In May 1944, the Venice Replacement Training Unit (F) was established at the base. This was simply an administrative move because the personnel had already been doing this job under the name of the Venice Fighter Pilot Training Unit. The mission remained the same, to train single engine pilots directly from advanced flying schools to become fighter pilots.

At the time (June 1944), the flight training curriculum was about 81 hours, which included aerial and ground gunnery, camera gunnery, dive and skip bombing, aerobatics, and cross country navigation. The ground school course was approximately 180 hours, with some of the subjects being: maintenance of aircraft armament, recognition of aircraft and naval vessels, medical procedures, fighter tactics, maintenance, Morse code, and combat intelligence. The actual number of training hours received by the pilots varied among groups being trained, depending upon the need for pilots at the time and other factors.

The training of the Service Groups and pilots was continually improved over the period the base was in operation. At first there were few training aids. The lesson plans were primitive (if at all), and the facilities to teach the students were very basic. This included outdoor classrooms, because of the lack of proper buildings. Over time, improvements were made as material and time permitted. A good example of this is the effort made to help the trainee pilots learn the complexity of

The former Officer's Club as it is today. Now it is used as a recreation center for a mobile home park. Inset: Bill Guyton was a fighter pilot with the 339th Fighter Group and trained at Venice. Here he is standing in front of the former Officer's Club.
(VENICE ARCHIVES AND AREA HISTORICAL COLLECTION)

the aircraft operations systems prior to actual flight in the airplane. Since the fighter planes had single seat cockpits and there was no room for an instructor, the student's first flight in his new plane was solo.

One of the training aids designed to help the pilot was called the Captivair. This new aid was put into use in April 1945—one month before the surrender of Germany. The Captivair was a P-51C that was anchored to the ground and in which the pilot could use all the controls to learn the proper engine startup and shutdown procedures, retraction of flaps, wheels, and the use of the radios etc.

Although Service Groups were still being trained at the base, other units including an Aviation Engineer Battalion, Sanitary Companies, and Provisional Aviation Squadrons also received training at Venice Army Air Field. By July 1944, the field's primary mission had become the combat training of fighter pilots.

While pilot training accidents (many fatal), were common at the base, an achievement of note was made in July 1944. The commander of the Replacement Training Unit, Lt. Col. William Hunt, received a commendation by the commanding officer of the III Fighter Command for the lowest monthly accident rate ever attained by a Group or unit assigned to the III Fighter Command. A total of 7,211 hours were flown that month, with just one accident. Probably a more representative view of the accident rate is the January thru May 1945 period, when the base had a total of 23 accidents and five men were killed. This may have been a particularly trying time for the training program because during this period the base was in the process of converting from the P-40, a type that had been in service since before the war, to the P-51 Mustang. The Mustang was one of the premier fighter aircraft of WW II, with performance far exceeding that of the P-40.

Bill Guyton recalls his training here for three months in late 1944. Following graduation he served with the 339th Fighter Group of the Eighth Air Force. His training was with the P-40 and he thought it was a good airplane, but not as good as the P-51 that he would fly in com-

Shortly after takeoff for a bomber escort mission on March 28, 1945, Bill Guyton's P-51 suffered engine failure as a result of a breakage in the throttle linkage. With considerable skill he was able to bring the aircraft down through a low overcast and make a rough but successful landing in an English field. Note the extensive damage to the aircraft including the missing right wing. (GUYTON)

Bill Guyton with his fellow pilots while taking training at Venice Army Air Field during October 1944. Bill is standing in the back row, second from the left. (GUYTON)

bat. While in training, he lived in a rented townhouse in Sarasota, which he recalls renting with his monthly housing allotment of $89.00. It was in the Officers Club that he proposed to his wife over the phone. The Officers Club building is still on the former base grounds, and today is used as a recreation building for a small mobile home park.

Following a series of organizational changes, the 13th Fighter Squadron was renamed Squadron O, and the 14th Fighter Squadron became

An aerial view of the hospital at Venice Army Air Field. A private hospital prior to the war it was converted to a station hospital after a considerable expenditure of time and money. (VENICE ARCHIVES AND AREA HISTORICAL COLLECTION)

Squadron T. As of the end of September 1944, Squadron O had 36 officers and 316 enlisted men. Squadron T at the same time had 64 officers and 365 enlisted men. The number of flight trainees assigned to the squadrons varied each month; however, in January 1945, each squadron was training 47 men. Squadron T was still using the P-40, and would switch over to the P-51 in February. By January, Squadron O was using 32 P-51s for its training program. During January 1945 there were 6,238 hours flown by the two squadrons.

Life was made a bit more pleasant for the enlisted men when in February 1945, two hundred and three POW's were assigned to Venice Army Air Field. The prisoners were assigned various manual labor details in the mess halls, and worked as labors and carpenters. Some worked in the Motor Pool and others were permanently assigned to maintain the kitchen, canteen and dispensary within their own confinement area. Also, some were used in the local agriculture industry.

The Sarasota Herald Tribune reported in its July 6, 1945 edition: "Using prisoners on private contract only when civilian labor is unobtainable and on army installations to release American soldiers for other duties, or for jobs for which civilian workers cannot be found, the working prisoners are paid 80 cents a day in canteen coupons—with a sharply curtailed list of items available." This comment was taken from a statement by Major Edward Brooks, commanding general of the Fourth Service Command that appeared in the article about the prisoners at Venice.

In a letter to the officer in charge of the German POWs at Venice AAF, written in May 1946, an ex-POW wrote: "Since I left Florida I have been often thinking of POW Camp Venice. It was a good place in every way. . . . You will have now a lot of work on your farm in Florida!"

One person who remembers the German POWs is Adele Cohill who saw them at the beach where they were employed at keeping the beach clean of debris such as seaweed.

In March 1945, a new base commander, Lt. Col. William Hunt formerly the Director of Operations and Training, assumed command of Venice Army Air Field, replacing Col. Vincent Dixon.

With the end of the war, training was slowed and attention turned to the eventual closing of the base. In October the base received notice that it would be placed on inactive status. Flying training ceased during the same month and arrangements were made to transfer the remaining P-51s to Hunter Field, Georgia. By early November, there was just one P-51 remaining on the field.

With the closing of the base, buildings were sold and put into other uses in the nearby area. One building became the city hall and another became the first Catholic church in the town. Adele Cohill's father bought one and converted it for use as a wash house by putting in the family's Maytag washer and hooking up the electricity and water.

5

Fighter Pilot Training

PAGE FIELD

In 1924, the city of Fort Myers, Florida, purchased a plot of land south of the city with the intention of developing it into a municipal golf course. It was never used for this purpose, but over time, and with continuing improvements, the site evolved into the Fort Myers airport. National Airlines began making regular flights into the airport in 1937, but soon discontinued many of the flights because of the poor landing conditions. Efforts to upgrade the facility were rewarded in January 1940, when the Works Projects Administration (WPA) started to build three concrete runways. In addition to the runways, other improvements were planned, and one year later the work was completed. By the time of Pearl Harbor, the airfield site had grown to about 618 acres, and had earned the nickname "Palmetto Field" because of the palmetto brush growing in and around the field. When the Department of War decided to utilize the airport, it leased the land from Lee County. The first lease was signed in February 1942, and later renewed in June 1944. At first, the USAAF called the field Fort Myers Army Air Base. The locals referred to the field by several different names including, Lee County Airport, Page Field, Fort Myers Airport, or Palmetto Field. The official name was Lee County Airport.

Eventually the field would be named Page Field to honor Captain Richard Page, a World War I aviator killed in a sea plane accident near Everglade, Florida in 1920. Captain Page was the first person from Florida to join the Aviation Section of the Signal Corps, the forerunner of the U.S. Air Force. Captain Page is credited with three German aircraft destroyed during World War I, and is a recipient of the Distinguished Service Cross, along with the *Croix de Guerre* and other awards.

The first group to train here was the famed 98th Bomb Group who arrived in March 1942 for training with the B-24 "Liberator" bomber. The Group spent about six weeks in training, which included flying anti-sub missions. They left on May 18 and were followed by the 93rd Bomb Group, which also trained with the B-24. In August 1942, the 336th Bomb Group (M) was activated at Page. In January 1943 the 53rd Fighter Group arrived at Page Field, and from this point on the field's major mission was the training of fighter pilots.

At the beginning of the field's existence, the living conditions were primitive, probably more so than at many of the other new training bases rapidly being established across the United States. Art Ferwerda, a member of the ground crew for the 93rd Bomb Group recalls:

Aerial photo of Page Field that was probably taken in the 70s. Note the swept wing aircraft on the ramp. Also of interest are the remaining revetments still in place along the taxiway between runways 5 and 13.
(FORT MYERS HISTORICAL SOCIETY)

Page Field as it appears today. The area in the middle of the right side of the photograph is the former cantonment area.

A general view of the former cantonment area, looking out the side window of an airplane. The air vent causes the distortion in the photo.

After our training was completed, and we were officially assigned and organized as the 93rd Bomb Group, everything was crated (like a circus) and we stood inspection. We were then shipped off to Fort Myers, Florida (Page Field) for advanced training prior to our deployment overseas.

I remember that whenever we traveled into a military base by train, we always took a spur siding, and traveled very slowly. This time, we were on the tracks that passed the warehouses that sorted and packed oranges. We would travel about a hundred yards and stop. A couple of times we stopped by one of these warehouses, and the people were out on the platform throwing oranges to us. We had so many oranges, that we didn't know were to put them.

The base at Fort Myers was very primitive. Once again we were living in tents. The ground was somewhat sandy, but very damp. We also had many mosquitoes; oh yes, and a few alligators too. The first two weeks at Fort Myers, we had no aircraft, so we were given menial tasks. I remember that about six of us would be selected every morning, to go down to the Fort Myers beach, which was nothing like it is today. There were no motels, etc. Just a few beer joints and eating places on stilts. We would fill the truck with

sand then spend the rest of the morning listening to the jukebox at "Nattie's Place" then return to the base, unload the truck, have lunch, and do it all over again in the afternoon. After we came back, we would eat our dinner, and take a shower, and then we most always would go into town. This didn't go on too long, because as soon as we started to get our assigned aircraft, all our time was spent on maintenance.

While in Florida the aircrews flew antisubmarine patrols over the Gulf of Mexico. During these patrols, the group was credited with destroying three U-boats. The ground maintenance crews also spent time working on the aircraft at night, which was to help us perform our duties during blackout conditions that existed in a combat zone. Of course because we were trained under tropical conditions, we were all convinced that we were going to be sent to the Pacific Theatre.

Fort Myers was a nice small town. Once we arrived it was overrun with military personnel; however, it still retained the original atmosphere. The airbase was about two miles from the town of Fort Myers, and the road leading into the town was just a two lane blacktop road, with just a few houses aside it.

As mentioned, the first group to train at Page Field was the 98th Bomb Group which flew the B-24 Liberator. The group arrived at the field on March 31, 1942 on about 18 rail cars of the Atlantic Coast Line and Seaboard Railroad. The Mayor of Fort Myers, Sam Fitzsimmons, and other dignitaries of the town, which at the time, had a population of about 10,600, welcomed the soldiers. This elite group was here until mid-May for training to accomplish a secret mission named Halpro. The mission's purpose was to bomb Tokyo using specially modified B-24 Ds based in China. At the time, the group's commander was Col. H. A. Halverson. Halpro was a combination of Halverson and project. The group did not bomb Tokyo but did participate in the low level bombing of the Ploesti oil refineries. Its leader, Col. John Kane, received the Medal of Honor for leading the group to the target despite the extreme danger of the oil fires already started, the delayed action bombs, and the alerted defenses.

One of the early problems facing the 98th Bomb Group was the Fort Myers sand that was used to fill the 100 pound practice bombs. When filled with the Fort Myers sand, the bombs weighed only 85 pounds. In order to give the bombs the correct weight, sand was trucked from Avon Park, located in mid-Florida.

The next group to train here was the 93rd Bomb Group, which arrived in May for further training with their B-24s.

Paul London, a member of the 93rd Bomb Group, remembers:

When the 93rd came to Page Field, I was assigned to work the Ft. Myers control tower with several other operators. We worked three shifts around the clock. The Ft. Myers tower was nothing more than a seven or eight-foot platform set on four wooden poles that were about fifteen feet high. We had so much equipment there was hardly room enough for two people. In addition to our flight operations, National Airlines had one

A postwar photo of a National Airlines plane on the ramp at Page Field. Note the cantonment area across the runway in the distance. (FORT MYERS HISTORICAL SOCIETY)

The bus, which was probably used for local transportation, parked at Page Field. (FORT MYERS HISTORICAL SOCIETY)

flight a day coming in, a fourteen passenger Lockheed Lodestar. We also controlled this flight through their station manager.

We lived in four man tents, and in the mess tent we ate standing up using our mess kits. The only other thing I remember are the mosquitoes. They would come out at 9 PM like clockwork. That's why we slept under mosquito netting.

Living conditions began to improve a little at Page Field when in July 1942, an arrangement was made to begin bus service from Fort Myers to the training field. Prior to this, the soldiers had to rely upon the good will of the people of Fort Myers for transportation to and from the city. Another major improvement to the morale of the troops was the announcement of the construction of an Enlisted Men's Service Club at the Yacht Basin located near the city. The soldiers from Buckingham Army Air Field, a huge gunnery-training center also located near Fort Myers, shared this facility.

Probably the biggest short-term improvement in living conditions was the construction of "hutments" that were to replace the tents the men currently lived in. The decision to build them was announced in July 1942. Hutments were small square wooden buildings that held about 6 to 8 men. Very basic in nature, they had no running water, or any other creature comforts. Still, they were probably a considerable improvement over the tents.

The early 1943, official history had this to say about the hutments:

Housing facilities were very poor. Dilapidated hutments were quarters for the enlisted men and were declared inadequate for occupancy for officers other than trainees. All officers, other than trainees lived off the base. . . . The Post Exchange consisted of a tumbledown converted hutment with dirt floor and snakes and rats visiting the building frequently. . . . About May 22 peticulosus humainus, otherwise known as bedbugs, started to overrun the field, attacking all enlisted men sleeping on the base. A steam chamber was set up, and all bed clothing, equipment, and hutments were thoroughly steamed, scrubbed, and made sanitary in an effort to overcome this plague. In approximately two weeks, the situation was well in hand. The mosquito problem was very acute at this time, and any person not sleeping under a mosquito net or having to work after sundown was seriously affected.

The chapel at Page Field. Probably the one converted from a barrack. Today it is a private residence.

Another comment on the living conditions was contained in this excerpt:

> Excessive rain during the month of June and very poor drainage conditions on the field resulted in practically every building being flooded. The hutments were of such poor condition that the inside of them was practically as wet as out-of-doors.

The last bomber group involved in training at Page Field was the 336th Bomb Group (M) that came from MacDill Field in August 1942. Their mission was to serve as a replacement training unit for B-26 crews; however, the group was here only a short time before moving to Avon Park Army Air Field in December. It was at this point that the base began to prepare for its long-term responsibility—training fighter pilots. One of the changes made to the base to prepare it for the new role was runway improvement.

The new year (1943) saw the 53rd Fighter Group arrive in January followed by their aircraft, the Bell P-39 Airacobra in February. This was the first fighter aircraft used for training purposes at Page Field. Later the base would use P-47s, P-40s and finally the P-51. The P-39 got mixed reviews from its pilots. Lacking a supercharger, it did not perform well at altitude, but was used early in the war because of the lack of better performing aircraft. The Russians used thousands of the P-39s, and loved them for their ruggedness, and ability to destroy ground targets, especially German tanks.

John Becket came to Page Field in April 1943 as an instructor and recalls: "The P-39 was a dangerous plane. I lost two classmates in Transition Training. It was a plane you had to fly all the time, you didn't want to do spins because the plane would tumble." John liked Fort Myers, the people were very hospitable, and would take you into their homes for dinner. As an officer, he was able to live off base, and it was in Fort Myers that he met his wife.

As mentioned, base housing was poor. Those who were able to live off base attempted to do so, but it was difficult for a number of reasons. The primary reason was the limited number of

A former firehouse. Note the location of the large doors that have been covered with new entrances and windows.

This structure was a latrine building that also contained several showers. The cadet officers probably used the structure. Today it sits behind a private residence. The overhang on the far end was a later add on. Below: The interior of the same building. Note the still existing WW II windows in the upper right corner.

rental units available. At the time, Fort Myers was a small town of about 10,000 people, whose population swelled in the winter due to the influx of tourists. Additionally, the 2,000 soldiers stationed at Page Field had to compete with the 16,000 soldiers stationed at nearby Buckingham Army Air Base. This was a large gunnery-training center that also had a significant number of soldiers and civilian workers eligible to live off base. Also, some dependents of the soldiers who were in training attempted to join them while they were stationed at the base, even though the military discouraged this practice. Many dependents still came to Fort Myers, and this only led to a greater demand for off base housing. The local city officials working with the military attempted to alleviate the situation, but it was difficult. In some cases, there were those who took advantage of the situation to maximize rental rates. Others were fair, and saw this as an opportunity to make the soldier's life a bit more pleasant by charging a reasonable rent. Sufficient housing was not the only concern; all the facilities were taxed beyond their capacity.

At this point (1943), Page Field was training fighter pilots. The mission of the field was to give additional training in fighter planes prior to the pilots being shipped to a combat unit. John Becket served at the field as an instructor for a few months in early 1943. This was a time when

fighter pilots were desperately needed throughout the Army Air Forces.

John recalls that the trainees were receiving about 80–90 hours flight training. The number of hours was based upon the need for fighter pilots. Some pilots received just 60 hours. The pilots were given orientation flights in a basic trainer, then the advanced trainer, the AT-6, and finally were checked out in the P-39. The major parts of their flight instruction included aerobatics, gunnery practice and formation flying. John was assigned three or four students and was responsible for them throughout their flight training.

With the production of fighter pilots in full swing, the strength of Page Field in January 1944 was 276 officers, and 1,393 enlisted men. One of the highlights of January was an impromptu appearance of Danny Kaye and Leo Durocher, who put on a show for the soldiers at the post theatre. The entertainers had driven to the base from Miami so they could entertain the troops. At the time, the fighter pilot trainees were using the Republic P-47 Thunderbolt. This aircraft was phased out over the next several months and replaced with the Curtiss P-40, a less capable aircraft. By May, 60 P-40s had replaced an equal number of P-47s. Other changes occurring in May were a field reorganization, which did away with the 53rd Fighter Squadron and substituted

were located here on a temporary basis for intensive training prior to moving overseas. One such unit was the 385th Service Group that had about 520 men, and arrived in September 1944. Other personnel were trained at Page Field's ground school, which was in addition to the aviation ground school given to the pilots undergoing training.

Page Field was a small training field when compared with the size and number of troops assigned to other training bases in operation throughout the United States. Many other training complexes had thousands of soldiers training on huge sites running into thousands of acres. The size and complexity of Page was a function of its training mission. Other training fields required more elaborate facilities. One example is the nearby Buckingham Army Air Field located about four miles east of Fort Myers.

Buckingham Army Air Field had a total area of 65,723 acres, and at its peak was home to about 16,000 men and women. There were about 700 buildings used to house and train the 50,000 gunners who graduated from the field. On the other side of the coin there were fields smaller than Page. One was Stout Field, near Indianapolis, Indiana, which sat on 357 acres and had about 130 buildings. This base was headquarters for the I Troop Carrier Command and was also a training base.

The small size of the field, combined with the need to operate efficiently, may have been one of the reasons why Page Field was a sub-base of MacDill Field. Later (March 1943), the training center became a sub-base of Sarasota Army Air Base. Still later, the field was a sub-base of Venice Army Air Field, and in October 1944 came under the jurisdiction of the Third Fighter Command. The relatively Spartan makeup of the field was probably a function of the base being under the command of other bases. As a result, Page Field did not receive the

Dean Reno standing at the entrance to the former officer's club.

the Page Replacement Training Unit (RTU.F). This was mostly an administrative move designed to make the training more efficient. At this time (June 1944), Page Field was a sub-base of Venice Army Air Base which was also in the business of training fighter pilots.

In addition to fighter pilot training, Page Field was also a training site for other units that same attention as a base operating under its own authority.

By late December 1944, the field's strength was 278 officers and 947 enlisted men. The graduating class of December 1944, consisted of 59 trainees who had flown 180 hours of flight training and had received 204 hours of ground school training.

Eventually, many concrete block buildings were constructed on the base, some of which were used to house the student officers. Other efforts to improve morale and living conditions continued with the construction of a base chapel in October 1944. The chapel was built in a converted barrack, with funds provided by the officers and civilian personnel. Many enlisted men volunteered their time to help provide the proper setting for the religious services that were formerly held in the post theatre. Because of local interest, the radio station WINK broadcasted the dedication of the chapel.

Late in the war (February 1945), German prisoners were assigned to Page Field to do manual labor and perform other details around the field. One of the several jobs assigned to the first 25 prisoners when they arrived was to build a stockade and prepare housing for about 200 more prisoners, due to arrive in March. The many onerous jobs done by the Germans were seen as a blessing for the enlisted men who were now relieved of some of these duties.

A significant change in the training program took place in March 1945 when the state of the art P-51 D was assigned to the field. This aircraft replaced the outdated P-40. There were several advantages in having the P-51 assigned to Page Field. Two of the most obvious were that the P-51 was a state of the art fighter and the pilots would be training on the same type of plane they would fly in combat. The trainers and trainees were delighted to get the modern aircraft.

The new aircraft was not seen as a blessing by the overworked ground crews, who had the responsibility to maintain the aircraft. The P-51 required different parts and different maintenance procedures than those used for the P-40. Also,

schooling would be required for the mechanics who would service and maintain the various systems of the P-51. At this time the maintenance workers were split into two shifts. The first shift started at 7:00 AM and worked until 2:00 PM. The next shift reported at 12:00 noon, and would work until no longer needed. The next day the shifts would change to insure the hours worked were balanced as fairly as possible.

As the war was coming to an end, and with the base about to close within the next few months, the first edition of the base newspaper was published. It was titled *Fighter Flashes*, and was first published on Wednesday March 21, 1945. The paper carried base events, sports, war news, and other items.

One article told about the three Hinkle brothers (Joe, Jene, and Jay), triplets from Walton, Indiana, who were temporarily assigned to Page Field for flying training. They were pictured standing in front of a P-51. This was probably the only

The Hinkle triplets, Joe, Jay, and Jene. They had the distinction of being 2nd Lieutenants, taking fighter pilot training, at the same base, at the same time in April 1945. Two flew combat in the south pacific, while the third remained in the United States in a training capacity. All returned safely from the war.
(MRS. JUNE HINKLE)

Messrs. Davidoff, DeBrino, Sutter, D'Agostino, Barett, and Basile standing outside their tent (#19) in June 1942. Photo is labeled left to right.

Above: 2nd Lieutenant Curt Keeler standing outside the Squadron T building. Note the crude construction, typical of the day. At right: Several soldiers standing outside a Theatre of Operations style building at Page Field.
(FORT MYERS HISTORICAL SOCIETY)

set of triplets in the Air Forces who were 2nd Lieutenants, taking fighter training at the same base, and at the same time. All graduated, Joe and Jene went to the South Pacific, and were based on Okinawa. Jay remained stateside. All three survived the war, and returned home to a more peaceful life.

By April 1945, when the Hinkle brothers were taking their flying training, the training program was more inclusive, and additional time was allocated to the program. Here's how the base history describes the activity at the time:

During the month the following types of training missions were flown, in accordance with III Fighter Command Regulations 50-50: formation—200' to high altitude; acrobatics—8000' to high altitude; navigation—low and high altitude; ground gunnery and strafing; aerial gunnery and bombing; camera gunnery exercises; night flying; fighter and bi-place instruments; combat tactics; group and squadron missions; homing missions and strange field landings; and maximum range, maximum throttle settings and minimum power missions.

Two views of a
former mess hall.

At the end of April, the field had a total of 127 aircraft, which included 56 P-40s. Even this late in the war, despite having more time and far superior facilities and instructors, training of fighter pilots continued to take lives. As an example, during the January to April 1945 period, there were 39 accidents in which six young men lost their lives

With the surrender of Japan, the process of shutting down training centers began in earnest all over the United States. Hundreds of training facilities were closed and put on inactive status. Page Field was no exception. The field received notice in early September that it would revert to inactive status in September. By September's end the plan was to have a total of 135 men on the field who

Today this building sits vacant. It was probably a barrack building in WW II. Several of this type structure were converted into single family homes after the war, and still serve this purpose today.

Several of the buildings that are found in the former motor pool area.

would prepare the facility for its closing. Toward this end, the ground school was stopped during the months of August and September. Those trainees who were in the last class were sent to other bases to complete their training. One class of trainees was transferred to Sarasota Army Air Field, and the other to Venice Army Air Field. By the end of September the field was quiet with just three aircraft remaining, an AT-6, a P-51, and a C-45.

Eventually Page Field reverted to civilian use. It served for many years as the major airport for the Fort Myers area. In 1983, with the opening of the Southwest Florida International Airport, Page Field's main role became that of a general aviation airport.

Even though WW II has been over for al-

most 60 years, there is much here at Page Field to remind the visitor of its proud service during WW II. Some of the student officers' concrete block buildings are still here and in use, many as private homes and apartments. The former officers' club is currently the home for a firm that makes sails for small boats, while the remaining warehouses are also being used for business purposes. The ball field is still in use, and some of the revetments may be seen along the runways. The chapel that came to being through the combined efforts of the officers, soldiers, and civilians of the area is in the same location where it was built in 1944. From time to time, a warbird will stop by, and for a short time, the field echoes with the sounds of the past.

6

From Farmland to an Air Base

LAURINBURG-MAXTON ARMY AIR BASE

To begin this chapter on an historical note, it's interesting to know that during the Civil War when General Blair's Corps (part of General Sherman's army) was making its march from Columbia, South Carolina to Raleigh, North Carolina, they marched over the same land that later would contain Laurinburg-Maxton Army Air Base.

The training center would be built in Scotland County, which is named after the early owners of the land, settlers from Scotland who fled their country after the battle of Culloden Moor in 1746. The heirs of Alexander and Mary Mckinnon who sold it to the government, owned part of the land on which the airbase was located. Another part of the land was purchased from Lizzie and Maggie Patterson, whose ancestors owned the land via a grant from the King of England. Over the years, the land had been used to raise cattle, cotton, tobacco, and food crops. In total, there were 37 landowners that had to part with their land in order to build the base. These parcels along with some land obtained from the cities of Laurinburg and Maxton, North Carolina gave the base a total of about 4,644 acres. The base was located about midway between the two cities, a short distance from U.S. Highway 74.

The cities of Laurinburg and Maxton were active in working with the War Department (today's Department of Defense), and the Civil Aeronautics Association (CAA) to have some kind of an airport built in their area. This was noted in the January 29, 1942 issue of *The Laurinburg Exchange,* that headlined, "Town and County Plan for Airport." At that time the two cities and the counties, Scotland and Robeson, were considering a jointly sponsored airport. The plan was to build the airport with local funds and money supplied by the CAA and the Works Progress Administration, (WPA). According to the newspaper: "The War Department would have control and use of the airport for the duration of the emergency, and the sponsors will be required to take over and operate the airport as a public airport at the end of the period."

Eventually, the War Department decided to build a training base located between the two cities. The decision was announced in the May 7, 1942 edition of The *Laurinburg Exchange* with headlines, "War Department Announces Great Air Base Development In County."

At the time of the announcement, work on the base had already started. Engineers were surveying the site, wells were being dug, a cemetery was in the process of being moved, and preparations

An aerial view of the site of the former Laurinburg-Maxton Army Air Base. During WW II, the base was spread out over 4644 acres and had about 567 buildings. Today it is the Laurinburg-Maxton Airport.
(SCOTLAND AERO SERVICES, INC.)

In the middle right of the photo are the two Butler hangars built in 1943 for the CG-4As. Below: A ground's eye view of one of the Butler Hangars. The structure at the end of the hangar is post-war construction. Still existing in the ramp area are many tie down hooks used to secure the gliders against wind damage.

A view of the parking ramps for the C-47s used in the tow operations of the base. Many are still visible off the taxiways of the runways. (SCOTLAND AERO SERVICES, INC.)

were under way to build a railroad line. The paper noted: " It is the biggest news locally that has broken in many a month. In fact it is so tremendous that it can scarcely be imagined not to say realized by the average individual."

But not everyone was happy with the decision to build the base. For some it meant moving off land that was their home. The heartbreak coupled with the willingness to make a sacrifice for our country is found in the letter sent by Mr. and Mrs. Sheppard to the president in May 1942. It read in part

> . . . the government is taking several places for an air base including our little place, and I was wondering if we could get just one little corner on which to live as it is on the out edge. They could not miss and it would be a great favor to us as we have worked so very hard for seven years to make our self and family a home. We love our home so very much we hate to leave the place. It was just a little forgotten spot when we took it over, and we have built it up all we could. But please understand sir, I could not complain at giving it up to the government if it is for

> defense for we are too glad to do all we can for our country. We have a son in the Navy and we are buying defense bonds through the plant at which we work . . .

The letter was answered by the Air Forces and explained why the land was needed and their "sacrifice is very much appreciated."

The new training base would be big, with its own sewer and water system, and about 567 buildings of all descriptions and sizes. Essentially it would become a city unto itself, bigger than its nearest neighbors, the cities of Laurinburg and Maxton. Laurinburg, the larger of the two towns, had a 1942 population of 5,727. The new training base was designed to house 10,000 people at full capacity. Clearly there was going to be a lot of flying at the new base; three runways were built each 150 feet wide and 6,500 feet long that formed a triangle with 510 acres of Bermuda grass in its center. Later, the center area would be used for glider landings.

Over the next several months as construction got underway, workers poured into the job

The former home of Mr. and Mrs. John Hamer. One of many in the city of Maxton that gave up their extra rooms for use by the civilian workers and later soldiers stationed at the airbase.
(MRS. PATSY HAMER)

site from all over the country. Grading for the runways and the buildings was in progress by June, and by the end of October 1942, most of the major construction was completed. During the peak of construction, there were about 6,000 workers rushing to complete the job. Most of the buildings were "Theatre of Operations" type temporary structures. These were frame type wooden buildings covered with black roofing paper on the sides and the roofs. They had no insulation of any kind, were heated by a pot bellied stove, and as a result, were cold in the winter, and without effective ventilation in the summer.

There were no adequate facilities to handle the sudden onrush of workers and other people connected with the base as they arrived in the area to work at the site. Workers felt lucky if they found a place to rent, even if it meant sharing their room with someone else. Eventually the government would build some civilian housing, but it was too little and too late.

One of the residents of the nearby town of Maxton is Pat Hamer, who was ten years old during the summer the base was built. She recalls:

> There were no motels, just one hotel in Maxton, and some tourist homes. There were six young men from Norwich University who stayed next door, and who took their meals at my house. At the same time, there were six young men from Clemson University who stayed at my house where they slept on the sun porch. They were engineering students who spent the summer work-

The home of Mrs. R. M. Morgan. She also opened her home to the construction workers and later the service men and their wives. The charge for a room was about $25.00 a week, not including meals.
(MRS. PATSY HAMER)

ing on the base. Since one group was from a northern school and the other from a school in the South, they fought the Civil War all over again. Times were still bad following the Depression, so my mother hired three cooks to prepare and serve meals to the construction workers as a way to increase the family's income. The workers were charged $1.00 for three meals a day, and $7.00 a week was charged for those who rented the four bedrooms in the upstairs of my home. The young men from the North were just fascinated with Southern cooking. The workers had to eat in shifts. The demand for sleeping space was so great that the day shift workers, who rented the rooms upstairs, would share the rooms with the night shift workers. After the construction was finished, and the workers moved on, the rooms were rented to soldiers and their wives. I still remember the names of some of the men and their wives.

While the base was under construction, its first commander, Colonel Y.A. Pitts, was on the scene helping to insure the construction and transition of the new training facility went smoothly. For a while, he and his wife stayed at the Cottonwood Hotel in Laurinburg.

One of the officers stationed at the base during its early period was Dr. Winston Tornow, who at the time was the base veterinarian. When he first got off the bus in the small town of Laurinburg, on October 2, 1942, he looked around and said "Oh, Lord, why me?" He had just finished spending time in Denver, and there was quite a difference between the two cities. Dr. Tornow remembers that Col. Pitts would ride horses frequently—there were about 16 horses used for patrol around the perimeter of the base. The Colonel always wore riding boots, and carried a small whip in his hand that he would strike frequently against his riding boots. Dr. Tornow thought the Col. was a fine person, very intelligent, and affable. The Col. and Dr. Tornow got along well together.

Colonel Pitts was instrumental in setting the tone for the base mission, and making sure it was carried out with enthusiasm and efficiency. He made certain that the base personnel understood that their reason for being there was to give the units in training the necessary service and assistance. According to the base history, the primary mission of the new training base was ". . . to furnish equipment, facilities, supplies, and protection to the Troop Carrier transport and glider troops taking training." These troops . . . "were

A view of runway 5/23 and its associated parking ramp. The Boeing 747s sitting at its far end indicates the size of the ramp.

81

Outdoor Mass is celebrated at the field. This may have been prior to the construction of the base chapels.
(RUFUS PITTMAN COLLECTION)

One of the former base chapels used by the men and women of Laurinburg-Maxton Army Air Base. Today it's in the same location and is the Skyway Baptist Church.

in their final stage of coordinated training with the airborne units of infantry, artillery, paratroop, engineer, and medical components of the Army."

The first Air Force training unit to arrive at the new base was the 317th Troop Carrier Group on November 6, 1942. This was followed in November and December by the first airborne unit to train at the base, the 88th Airborne Infantry. They would be followed by 40 different organizations through August 1943. Included were many units of the 82nd and 101st Airborne Divisions.

It was customary for the men of the training center to put on military exhibitions for various visitors and dignitaries who came to the field. General Arnold, commanding general of the U.S. Army Air Forces, dropped in on the base in April 1943, and was accompanied by Air Vice Marshal Foster of the British Royal Air Force. Treated to a display of military prowess by the 82nd

Airborne Division and the First Troop Carrier Command, the general left the field with a talk to a small group of men saying, "I want to thank you men for a most impressive and interesting demonstration." He would return just a few months later in August on a visit of much greater importance.

This time his visit would be crucial to the future of the entire glider pilot training program and the airborne concept. This would be a special two-day tactical demonstration of night and day glider and airborne capabilities. The General was accompanied by about 300 military

Reception line of a party celebrating the 1st anniversary of the opening of Laurinburg-Maxton Army Air Base. (RUFUS PITTMAN COLLECTION)

as noted in Gerard Devlin's book, *Silent Wings:*

General Marshall ordered a select board of officers convened to determine methods of improving glider and parachute troop operating procedures. . . . At the same time, Marshall directed the Army Air Forces to conduct extensive maneuvers with glider troops and technical tests of the CG-4A glider at the newly completed Laurinburg-Maxton Army Air Base in North Carolina.

Further complicating this issue was the crash (in full view of civilian and military personnel) of a CG-4A at Lambert Field in St. Louis. This was just three days before the planned demonstration at Laurinburg-Maxton on August 4. The glider flight at Lambert was to be a publicity event. Aboard the glider, among other well known personnel, was the Mayor of Saint Louis. The glider was towed aloft normally, but after gaining altitude and after being released from its tow plane, the glider's wing broke away from the fuselage. The glider plunged down nose first in full view of the audience, and slammed into the ground nose first. There were no survivors. The picture of the crash and the story received wide coverage in the news. Later investigation revealed a faulty part had caused the wing to separate from the fuselage.

observers. News personnel were invited and were allowed to photograph and file stories on some of their observations.

The reason for the visit was a memo written by General Eisenhower to General Marshall (Army Chief of Staff), following the invasion of Sicily in July 1943. While the invasion of Sicily resulted in victory, the loss incurred by the glidermen and the airborne troops they carried or dropped over the island was horrific. The alarm was caused not by losses in ground fighting, but by the terrible toll taken by the men, their gliders, the C-47s that towed them, and equipment. These losses were the result of weather, poor training, bad communications, friendly fire, and the dropping of paratroopers (and the landing of gliders) far from the intended areas. Following this action, General Eisenhower decided that there should be no division-size airborne units in the United States Army. Part of his memo stated: "I do not believe in the airborne division." He believed the units were too large to be effectively controlled, and would be scattered over too wide an area.

Before taking the steps suggested by General Eisenhower, General Marshall did the following

The Post Theatre. The movie playing at the time was "East Side of Heaven." (SKYWAY BAPTIST CHURCH)

A partial view of Skyway Terrace. Built to help ease some of the housing shortage, it remained in use following the closing of the base. It eventually became a low-income housing project and was eventually torn down. (SKYWAY BAPTIST CHURCH)

These events and others were on the General Arnold's mind as he arrived at the training base. Accompanying General Arnold were numerous officials that included General Swing, head of the board convened by General Marshall. Also along was Major General Chapman, who was the commanding general of the Airborne Command. Over the next two days, the group was treated to a spectacular show that demonstrated the impressive combat abilities of the glider. This included the transport of troops and equipment into landing areas, and even a flight to simulate an emergency glider landing on the lake at the base named, "Lee's Mill Pond." More was to come.

The most impressive, and perhaps the most dangerous demonstration, was a landing by six gliders in an isolated area of the base in virtually total blackout conditions. Only a handkerchief-shrouded flashlight was used to guide the gliders to their landing area. The base newspaper *The Slipstream* reported that ". . . General Arnold remarked, and he grinned as he told how an 'invading' glider force had surprised him on this very field . . . even though he was expecting it. . . . Trained military observers expressed amazement at the eerie precision of the maneuver. . . . It was almost impossible to see the gliders in the air, even at less than 300 feet despite a brilliant background of stars."

Another landing was held the following night. This time one glider, along with others, carried 11 members of the base band. This ship would be the last to land, and as it was still in the air began playing "Coming In On A Wing and a Prayer." The music started at 5,000 feet over the field and was followed by "The Army Air Corps" and "Blue Skies." Just as the glider was about to land among the scattered timber,

This structure was a base firehouse and later converted to another use following the field's closing.

the band finished by playing "What the Hell Do We Care!" One solider remarked " Sounds like a parade up there—of angels."

Later in remarks General Arnold would note "The men here today, are receiving 50% more training than those who landed in Sicily." He also wrote in a letter to Col. Pitts dated August 26:

The work accomplished at your base, which resulted in the very successful glider demonstrations there on August 4, and particularly the night operation of August 3 is most pleasing to me and I desire to commend you and the members of your staff for their noteworthy efforts. I consider that more had been accomplished toward making the glider a potent weapon of war during the preceding month than during any other like period. The techniques demonstrated to me had many times been reported as impossible, and I hope and expect they will now be expanded to such an extent that they will play a vital part on our final victory.

Inside view of the commissary store showing soldiers and others shopping for their groceries. While appearing to be spartan, it was not that unusual from the average grocery store of the day.
(RUFUS PITTMAN COLLECTION)

An interior view of the Quartermaster office. Note the fan in the extreme right corner, the open door and window and the low ceiling. During the summer months, the heat and humidity must have made working conditions most uncomfortable. (RUFUS PITTMAN COLLECTION)

Clearly these demonstrations, especially the night landings, had impressed the visitors. They did much to restore confidence following the errors made in the landings at Sicily just one month before.

During the months of March to June 1944, the base underwent several major changes. Some of the changes included new commanding officers, and a change in the base's mission. On March 29, Colonel Loyd Sailor replaced Colonel Pitts. Col. Reed, Jr., quickly replaced Col. Sailor and by mid July, he had been replaced by Lt. Col. Ellsworth Curry. It was during this period that a major base reorganization took place.

The new mission for Laurinburg-Maxton was to train student officers in advanced glider techniques and ground fighting. Also important in the new training program was the training of C-47 pilots, who were probably already rated C-47 pilots, but would receive further training in the towing of gliders. Colonel Curry was well qualified to carry out this new training program. Prior to this assignment, he had been at Bowman Field, Kentucky, and was instrumental in the training of student officers at the Glider Crew Training Center at Bowman Field. Col. Curry had over 7000 hours of flying time, and was Director of Operations and Training at Laurinburg- Maxton before assuming command of the base. The first glider pilot training class arrived on June 2, 1944, just four days prior to the invasion of Normandy.

At this point it's probably best to briefly describe the CG-4A for those not familiar with the aircraft. The CG-4A was, by the standards of the day, huge. The Waco Aircraft company was the design contractor and it along with 15 other

This is Lee's Mill pond. The body of water was the site for many training exercises on the proper way to leave a glider in the event of a ditching. It was drained in April 1945, the reason for which remains unclear.

companies, produced about 14,000 of the gliders. The aircraft could carry 13 fully equipped soldiers, a jeep with four-man crew and equipment, or a 75mm howitzer and crew plus supplies and ammunition. It had a wingspan of over 83 feet and weighed almost 4,000 lbs. when empty. While simple in appearance, the final versions of the glider had over 70,000 parts. It was made of metal tubing, canvas, and wood, and was generally towed into the air by C-47s. Ford Motor Company produced the most CG4-As, building over 4,000 gliders at their Kingsford production facility in northwestern Michigan. Pilots spoke well of the glider; it was relatively easy to fly and very forgiving in flight.

The student pilots who reported to Laurinburg-Maxton had already received extensive training in flying the CG-4A, and while at the field would receive advance glider training, which included extensive combat training. By this time (April 1944), the war had turned in the Allies favor. Many hard lessons had been learned, and these would be put to use in the advanced training program. The invasion of Europe, in which huge numbers of gliders would be used, was just three months away.

In addition to the training of glider pilots, considerable additional training was done with C-47 pilots and other groups; however, the major portion of the training resources were directed toward the glider pilot program. The emphasis of this new training curriculum was to improve flying skills (especially at night) and train the pilots to be highly capable infantrymen.

The program evolved during the months of April, May and June. It was broken down into Ground and Flying Training, and Military Training. Some of the subjects covered during this period of Ground and Flying Training included weight and balance, meteorology (both added in June), loading and lashing, radio code, glider pilot duties, and pre-flight familiarization. Flying training included take off and landing, flying the CG 4A while it was under tow, and lots of night flights.

One of the more interesting and sometimes frightening techniques taught at Laurinburg-Maxton (not necessary at all times or to all students), was the "snatch pick-up." The technique was utilized following the invasion of Normandy and the invasion of Holland, when it was critical to salvage as many CG-4As as possible for further use. The technique also saved many lives

This unusual structure was (and still is) used as a water reservoir by the base. Essentially it is a large covered swimming pool.

A view of a few buildings of the base hospital. The large units on the roof of the building in the left of the picture are cooling units. A luxury for the day, they typically were used to help with the oppressive heat in those buildings that were used for the more important purposes, i.e., operating suites. (SKYWAY BAPTIST CHURCH)

when the glider would be loaded with wounded and "snatched" from locations where runways did not exist. One of its earliest combat uses was in Burma during April 1944.

The "snatch" system worked like this: Two poles resembling football goal posts were set up about 50 yards ahead of the glider that was to be picked up. One end of the nylon towline was attached to the glider nose and the other end was hung between the two poles in front of the glider. There the towrope would be "snatched" by the hook of an arm extending from the tow plane, as it flew just few feet above the ground and over the glider.

George Theis who served as a member of the 440 Troop Carrier Group, 98th Troop Carrier Squadron, and as a CG-4A pilot, recalls his training that included the "snatch pickup." George recalls:

Prior to establishing the training school at Laurinburg-Maxton, the early glider pilot program was very disorganized and haphazard. I received my basic glider training at Wichita Fall, Texas (Sheppard Field) in a PT-19 simulating power-off landings. I arrived at Laurinburg-Maxton in late October 1944 for advanced tactical training after graduating from South Plains Army Air Field, in Lubbock, Texas. It was there that I first flew

the CG-4A. The tactical training at the Laurinburg-Maxton included learning glider snatch pickup. To prevent stalling the glider, I would grab the cross member (next to the pilot's seat) with my left hand while holding the wheel with my right hand. This prevented me from being thrown back because of the force of the pick up. We also had night flying, when we would be released from the tow plane, and fly back to land on a simulated runway lined with two or three flare pots. Landing in the "Pea Patch" at the field involved landing between obstacles. They dug holes and planted tall trees in the front and rear of the "Pea Patch." As skill progressed, the distance between the trees became shorter and shorter. (They would move the trees). I think the CG-4A was a very maneuverable aircraft and after the war, during an air show in Germany, I looped one.

The "Pea Patch" referred to by George Theis was a large open area on the south side of the base, the west end of which was conveniently located near the base hospital.

Another glider pilot who was trained in the "snatch pickup" was Gale Ammermon, who received this training in Europe following Operation Market-Garden. Gale had flown the GC-4A in the Normandy Invasion, and had just finished flying in Market-Garden. Gale would also fly a

CG-4A in Varsity, the airborne assault across the Rhine River in March 1945. Here's how he describes part of this "snatch" training in his excellent book, *An American Glider Pilot's Story:*

> The instructor signaled the ground crew that he was ready, and the ground crew signaled the C-47. The C-47 pilot took off, went around the field about a quarter of a mile from the airport boundary. The pilot lined the C-47 up with the glider and the pick-up poles, and started a long gentle dive toward the glider. As the tow plane approached, the roar of the two big Pratt and Whitney engines was overwhelming. As the C-47 roared over the glider it shivered, danced and vibrated like a thing alive. The hook caught the tow line on the two poles, the CG-4A leaped into the air, dust and debris flew in every direction, and as though by magic, the glider was scooting, gaining speed and altitude. In a few seconds the CG-4A went from standing still on the ground to a speed of 120 miles per hour a hundred feet above the ground.

During this period (May 1944), there were three auxiliary fields in use at Laurinburg-Maxton. The fields were located at Lumberton, Rockingham, and Knollwood, North Carolina. Of interest is the training done with the CG-13A, at Lumberton. The CG-13A was a larger capacity glider of which only 132 were made. The number available for training at this time was limited to only four, and of these, one was damaged in a landing accident, and the other destroyed in a crash that took three lives. Later in January 1945, there was considerable training

One of the few derelict buildings remaining from World War II. This one is located in the maintenance complex near the Butler hangars.

with the glider at Camp Mackall, which was located near Laurinburg-Maxton. The flying training with the CG-13A was switched to Camp Mackall because the flying field at Laurinburg-Maxton was saturated with GG-4A training.

The military training of the glider pilots was extensive; the base history called it "the finest in the world." That may be a bit of an exaggeration but it was thorough, and structured to insure the glider pilot's ability to fight with the infantry once he had landed his glider in the combat zone. The pilot's responsibility was to report, as soon as possible after landing, to an area where he could be transported back to fly again; however, sometimes this required he fight with the Infantry.

The training was divided into three parts, Weapons, Tactics, and General Subjects. Some of the weapons training included: firing the Carbine, the "Bazooka" Rocket Launcher, the Sub-Machine Gun, the mortar, and hand and rifle grenades. Some of the Tactical Training encompassed night problems, and the construction of roadblocks. The General Subjects classes taught (among other things), the use of maps and the compass, booby traps, camouflage, and physical training. Since the training curriculum was constantly changing, based upon learnings from combat and new tactics, not all classes received the same training. For example, Class 44-8 was the first to receive extensive training in reorganization tactics used by the pilots after they had landed in a hostile area. Much of the new teaching was learned from the glider pilots who participated in the invasion of France.

Another glider pilot who took advanced training at Laurinburg-Maxton, and would later be shipped out to the Pacific in late 1944, is Charles Anderson. He recalls a night compass reading course while in training:

> One night, a friend and I were assigned the problem of finding a certain location using compass heading as a guide. To do this we had to travel on a certain compass heading for a number of yards, than a different heading for a specific distance, and do this several times, all of this was supposed

to lead to a specified point. Rather than go to all this trouble, we figured out on paper where the headings and distances would lead. Then we just walked directly to the point. The point just happened to be near a farmer's watermelon patch. So we just sat down, and waited at this point while enjoying some of the farmer's watermelons. Later the farmer complained, but there was little our superiors wanted to do with us this late in our training. I had a lot of confidence in the CG-4A, and thought it was well built and flew well.

This intensive training was not without cost in human lives, injuries, and damage to gliders. As an example, during May 1944, there were 10,272 glider landings, and 348 gliders were damaged, not all from landing, but most due to pilot error. Since the training was designed to simulate combat conditions, many of the landings occurred in close and confined spaces and others at night. Engine failure, on the tow ship, generally a C-47, created an especially hazardous condition for both the tow ship and the glider. One night in May 1944, a tow ship had an engine failure while it was pulling two gliders. The towrope was released and one rope, dangling from a glider, got caught in the trees, causing the glider to crash. This resulted in the death of one officer and injury to two others. Later in the same month, a tow plane drifted back into the path of the gliders it had just released, when the tow plane's trailing towrope sheared off a wing of a glider. Two Flight Officers were killed in the crash that followed. The most serious accident in the last half of 1944 occurred when all 12 men in a C-47 were killed following the crash of their plane. Parachutes and supply bundles hitting their plane after the equipment was dropped from a higher flying plane caused the crash. The group of planes that contained the one that dropped the bundles had become lost during a night formation from the Lumberton auxiliary field. The group was out of place, and did not drop the equipment at the proper time. It did not see the lower formation because of poor visibility and the lack of navigation lights.

Class 44-8 (August 1944) provides an example of some causes of glider damage. Three of the most common accidents and the resultant damage to the gliders were caused by hard landings, making a landing approach to close to the ground, and landing tail first.

The training of the glider pilots and the troops they carried was often done on a massive scale that extended over hundreds of miles of airspace and many different locations. A good example of this training is reported in *The Hamlet News Messenger* of December 2, 1943.

The paper reported: "This week's maneuvers will attempt to show that glider troops as well as parachute troops can be flown great distances to their objectives, can be landed at the intended spots in large numbers and can get along on supplies ferried in subsequently by Troop Carrier Command planes." In an operation similar to the Normandy Invasion that would take place just 6 months later, more than 1,900 paratroopers were dropped near the "enemy" airfield defended by 700 men. This was just one phase of the tactical problem. In another part of the mock invasion, gliders carrying full loads of men and supplies flew over 200 miles of simulated ocean before landing on their assigned fields in "enemy" territory. Much of the training occurred at night over a 2,500 square mile maneuver area in the sand hills of central North Carolina. In one phase of the exercise about 6,000 men and their equipment were moved by air in about two hours time at night. Two men were killed and 49 others injured in this night exercise. The paper reported that this was the largest night maneuver to date, and was the first time an entire airborne division was used. Hamlet, then a small town, located about 20 miles northwest of the training field, blacked out its lights at night as part of the invasion exercise.

Training of the glider pilots continued as it was developed in April 1944, but with continuous modifications of techniques and facilities. At this time (July 1944), it was an 8-week program. Some of the added subjects included were tank hunting by small combat teams, jungle reconnaissance, and glider pilot reorganization after landing in enemy territory. Of interest is the addition of the study of weapons and battle habits of Japanese soldiers. Also during this period, a glider

Dr. Winston Tornow standing next to the Laurinburg-Maxton Memorial plaque which was dedicated on November 11, 1989. Dr. Tornow is a veterinarian and for part of the war was stationed at the base. The plaque sits in a prominent location next to the modern terminal building located on the former air base. It reads: "In memory of the combat glider pilots and other airborne assault personnel who trained at the Laurinburg-Maxton Army Air Field during World War II. This memorial is dedicated to the brave young Americans, especially to those who in large numbers gave their lives in defense of freedom during the bloody airborne operations of World War II. The Laurinburg-Maxton Army Air Field was one of the major combat glider training bases in America between October 1942 and April 1945, during World War II."

ditching training facility was set up in Lee's Mill Pond, a large body of water located on the base. In the pond, a C-47 mock up fuselage was built, which gave the troops an opportunity to launch and retrieve the glider used in the ditching training.

The reader will gain some idea of the intensity of training by looking at the number of landings made by the 198 graduates of Class 44-8 (August 1944). Each student made an average of 48 landings for a total of 9,542 landings for the class. Another class (44-12) that graduated on January 11, 1945 made 14,610 landings, which was an average of 55 landings per student. During the period that saw six classes graduate, (August, 1944–January 1945) 1,114 students were graduated from the glider pilots' training school.

During the time (mid to late October 1944), a special training class was given to 298 power pilots to teach them to fly the CG-4A. For the most part, these pilots had earned their wings as rated power pilots, and were not happy at the prospect of flying the ungainly CG-4A. Additional classes would contain power pilots and generally their attitude was the same, that of resentment with flying gliders.

The training of the glider pilots was constantly affected by many factors including, weather, equipment availability, other training requirements, and the distractions caused by supporting military maneuvers. As an example, Class 44-8 was effected by two major events, the first a severe windstorm, and the other was

the need to preserve gliders for the combined Airborne-Troop Carrier maneuvers scheduled for September. The windstorm was particularly troublesome because of the extensive damage to the gliders and training facilities.

The storm, which hit late in the afternoon of July 28, 1944 was especially powerful with winds up to 95 miles per hour. Actually, the wind force may have been stronger because during the storm the base weather station's anemometer was broken. Those gliders not tied down were lifted by the wind and carried through the air only to crash into the ground or into buildings. Some of those that were tied down suffered damage after being banged into one another. Following the storm, and after things had calmed down, a survey of the damage was made several days later. In addition to the damage to the base facilities, there was a total of 384 gliders damaged, 140 of which were beyond repair. The number of gliders damaged gives an indication of the large quantities of planes used at Laurinburg-Maxton. In early January 1945, in addition to the gliders, there were about 39 C-47s assigned as well as other aircraft, including C-46s, several smaller Piper Cub type planes, and small numbers of other aircraft.

With the end of the war (August 1945), training at the base ceased, and as the history states ". . . leaving Laurinburg-Maxton without any known mission." Colonel Curry, the commanding officer since July 1944 was discharged from the service in August, and returned to work for a civilian airline. Lt. Col. Lloyd Long, who ten days later was replaced by a different commanding officer, replaced him. Activity began to diminish, and as people were discharged from the service or transferred to other bases, the former thriving military complex slowly began to take on the appearance of a ghost town. By September, there were 3,726 members of the military assigned or attached to the field, and at the end of August the number of civilians working at the field had dropped to 914.

With the base closed and training stopped, it was converted to other uses. The base hospital served as the Scotland Memorial Hospital until a hospital was opened in another location. Several buildings were moved from the field and converted to other uses, and others went to the nearby town of Maxton where a few are still being used as homes. The chapel is still on the site of the old base, and today is the Skyway Baptist Church.

From time to time, the Army's elite parachute team, the Golden Knights, still uses the facilities just like their predecessors did so many years ago. Several buildings remain, including the large "temporary" Butler hangars built in 1944. If you drive down one of the still existing, but mostly forgotten former base streets, you will find many remains of the old buildings, now almost obscured by over 50 years of brush and pine tree growth. Lee Mills Pond is still here and can easily be seen from the air, as can the many individual aircraft parking pads located near the ramps. The ramps still have the aircraft tie down anchors embedded in the concrete.

The former training center is today a growing industrial park with an active airport of two runways, one of which is 6,489' long and 150' wide. Located in the modern terminal building are the offices of Randy Hoffman and John McRae, owners of the Scotland Aero Services. They operate a flight school, and are deeply interested in preserving the history of this base. Just outside the building is a 24" by 30" bronze plaque mounted on a five foot tall by three feet wide granite slab that honors the memory of the glider pilots and other airborne assault personnel who trained at the base. The memorial was dedicated on Veterans Day 1989.

Nature is slowly reclaiming parts of the former air base.

A circa 1942 view of the main entrance to Williams Field. In the distance to the left is the post chapel and directly behind in the distance is the base headquarters. (TOM KELLY)

Below: The same spot as seen today. Note the flagpole, probably in the same location as it was in 1942. (TOM KELLY)

"Willie"

WILLIAMS AIR FORCE BASE

Williams Air Force base was one of the larger training bases built during the frantic expansion of the Army Air Forces just before World War II. This base would serve proudly throughout that war and well into the 1990s.

At first, no one was quite sure what to call the place. To some it was the Mesa Military Airport, to others Higley Field. Some early newspaper accounts referred to it as the Air Training Base near Higley. Eventually the base was named Williams Field to honor 1st Lt. Charles L. Williams, a West Point graduate and a native of Arizona. Lt. Williams served in World War I and later was killed when his aircraft plunged into the sea off Oahu, Hawaii on July 6, 1927. On January 14, 1942, the War Department made the name official. In 1945 his brother, Col. Robert Williams, would visit the field. Col. Williams was on his way to Fort Sam Houston where he was to assume responsibility as Surgeon of the Fourth Army.

During March 1941, some citizens of Mesa, Arizona (about 13 miles north and west of the base) were actively working toward getting an Air Corps facility located near their city. One of the sites seriously considered for the new base was on the Gila River Indian Reservation located about six miles west and a mile south of Chandler, Arizona. Later a different spot was chosen that was about seven miles east of Chandler. At that time, the land on which the base would eventually be built was vacant and not used for agriculture because of a lack of irrigation. It had no homes or farms and was essentially desert with a few Indian ruins scattered about.

The information gathered by the officials of Mesa showed that the area under consideration would be an excellent location for a training base of some kind. The water supply was good (there were already two wells on the property); it was close to the Southern Pacific Railroad, and near an excellent road system. Housing was considered to be adequate for the influx of construction workers that would be required to build the base. Actually, it was probably not adequate but this was typical of most new bases. The area around the proposed base probably offered better than average housing conditions because of the nearby towns of Chandler, Gilbert, and Tempe. Also, Phoenix was nearby. Eventually the information was sent to the War Department (Department of Defense) in the hope that the military would establish a base on the location.

On their own initiative, the city fathers of Mesa began to acquire rights to the property that

Aerial view of Williams Field as it is today. (TOM KELLY)

was under the ownership of at least 33 different owners. Agreement was reached with the railroad to build a spur line to the location, and arrangements were made for the appropriate electric, telephone and gas needs. The city agreed to lease the land to the government for $1.00 per year.

The hard work paid off with the announcement in June 1941 by the mayor of the city of Mesa (George Goodman) that the War Department had approved the site for an air base. At the time, there were about 2,610 acres in the area being considered for the new base. The announcement noted: "It is requested that you acquire the land for lease to the Government as expeditiously as possible." The official history talks about the early contracts (June 1941), one for a well and another for elevated water tanks.

The June 20 and June 27, 1941 issues of *The Chandler Arizonan* made public the fact that a new base would be built near the city of Chandler. In the June 27th issue, the paper reported "Boosting the outlay from the initial sum of

$2,500,000 to $4,772,374 the War Department officially authorized a Basic Flying School nine miles east of Chandler, Monday." It went on to say, "One thing is certain, the field will be a permanent Army Air Base, and with a little time may develop into the ranking center for air flight training in the United States. The climate is favorable and there is plenty of room for expansion." To put some perspective on the field's 4.8 million dollar price tag, in today's economy (2002), that would be about 60 million dollars.

At about the same time as construction was authorized for Williams Field, other major airfield projects in the same area were being planned or were already in the process of construction. One was Luke Field about 45 miles north and west of Williams Field. Other Air Forces training fields in the vicinity included Thunderbird Airport #1, Thunderbird Airport #2, Falcon Field, and a Navy training field later taken over by the Air Forces and called Coolidge Army Air Field. Coolidge Army Air Field would serve as sub-base for Williams Field.

Higley was the town nearest to the new training base and was described in the publication *Willy Field Happenings during World War (Believe Them or Not)*, as a small crossroads community with a gas station, grocery store, and a house or two. Higley was about two miles west of the field.

As of December 10, 1941, the field still had no official name, and the mailing address was changed to Headquarters Air Corps Advanced Flying School #7, Chandler, Arizona. This was three days after the start of World War II. In the preceding October, Major Bridget, who was the field's Project Officer and first Commanding Officer, went to the Mesa Chamber of Commerce to get their suggestions for names of the new base. They recommend the following: Mesa Airbase, Rothrock Field, and Stewart Field. Also under consideration at that time were Williams Field and Wirz Field.

The first meal was served in the mess hall on December 4, 1941. Before this, the enlisted men either ate at a "cook shack" (a construction com-

Cadet Eugene Geiger at the "Wishing Well." Cadets tossed coins into the wishing well to bring them luck in their future assignments.
(MESA SOUTHWEST MUSEUM)

pany dining facility) located on the field or traveled into Chandler to eat. The first dinner included, roast beef, dressing, mashed potatoes, gravy, cabbage salad, peaches, coffee, and canned milk. Drinking water was trucked into the field from Higley on a daily basis. Showers were taken in the high school gymnasium located in Chandler about ten miles from the field. The key used to get into the school was kept at an eating and drinking establishment called the Western Tavern. Some men were given permission by Major Bridget to use his staff car to drive to the school for their showers, but he insisted the car not be parked in front of the Western Tavern. Living conditions became a bit more tolerable around December 5, 1941, when at least one of the barracks had water and electricity connections completed.

Early conditions were tough. The dust on the field was very fine, three to six inches deep, and turned into a gooey mess when it rained, making driving very difficult if not impossible in spots. Vehicular traffic had to go very slowly because the excessive dust created would severely limit visibility. Dust devils (or miniature cyclones) were common, and several could be seen at the same time across the field.

The number of men assigned to the training

A line up of AT-6s on the ramp. Note the Williams Field name on the cowl. In 1943 there were approximately 348 aircraft at Williams including about 237 AT-6s. (MESA SOUTHWEST MUSEUM)

field grew slowly and by early December 1941, there were 402 men on the post.

The unit history describes the condition on the field just after the bombing of Pearl Harbor:

> The entire field was scarred with ditches for utilities, gaping pits intended for field storage tanks, and the foundations for buildings under construction. Moving about the unlighted post at night was hazardous especially when the ditches, some of them as much as eighteen feet in depth, became filled with water from flash floods. During the dry days a cloud of fine dust hung over the entire cantonment through which bulldozers and trucks made their way with difficulty.
>
> Within the buildings, work went on under great difficulties because of the lack of equipment. Crates served as desks and various makeshift arrangements had to supply other needed furniture. ... A trip to the mess hall meant either wading through knee-deep dust or ploughing through equally deep mud, depending upon the state of the weather. ...

Construction continued into 1942, although in January and February there was little done because of the mud caused by rain. At one point in early 1942, much of the new base was under water. One project not paid with government funds was the construction of the base swimming pool, finished in June 1942. The pool, the idea of now Colonel Bridget, was built by the officers and enlisted men of the base during their spare time at night and during the day. Resources to help build the pool came from the citizens of the nearby communities as well as the winter residents of the San Marcos Hotel in the nearby town of Chandler. The pool was much appreciated by everyone on the field, especially since the extreme heat of summer could cause the temperature to rise to 120 degrees inside a building by mid-afternoon.

Another morale builder for the soldiers at Williams Field was the early construction of the base theatre. The base was somewhat isolated

The amphitheater also called the "shell" and a view of the surrounding area. The shell was built in 1942 and was used for graduations, performances, USO shows and concerts. It had a seating capacity of about 300. Inset: A view of the remains of the foundation for the amphitheater. (TOM KELLY)

and transportation into the nearest town was difficult, so a base theatre, soon followed by a second, was completed in mid-December 1941. A good indication of the popularity of the theatre is its attendance through 1942—190,334 people. A second theatre opened in October, and by the end of December had attracted 42,477 patrons. The first movie shown at the theatre was *Birth of the Blues* with Bing Crosby, Mary Martin, and Rochester. The theatres were also used for other purposes such as meetings, class lectures, showing of training films, and graduation ceremonies. The first class to hold a graduation ceremony in the new theatre (#2) was Class 43A, after which the officers attended a dinner at the officers Club, the dinner menu included barbecued spareribs.

Another form of entertainment was the occasional visits of well-known and not so well known entertainers and celebrities who performed for the soldiers stationed at the field. Probably the best known were Bob Hope, Bing Crosby, Jerry Colonna, and Francis Langford who entertained 3500 people in a packed hangar in early 1943. Later Spencer Tracy visited

A partial view of "Willie's Beer Hangar" taken in July 1944. This was a favorite spot for cadets to relax. Pictured from left to right are Cadets Ed Wnuk, Don Wideman, and Leland Wilson. Note the cadet patch on the sleeve of their shirt. (MESA SOUTHWEST MUSEUM)

the base to study a P-38 for his movie, *A Guy Named Joe.*

Others included Hank Greenberg, the famous baseball player of the time, who visited the field as part of his tour of Air Force fields.

By July 1942, the base was fully involved in

This WW II scene shows a base chapel and what was probably a post theatre to its right. The remaining buildings were enlisted men's barracks. (TOM KELLY)

The base was closed in 1994 and is slowly being converted into an industrial park. It is the major airport for the Phoenix area. This scene shows a part view of the terminal building with a WW II hangar alongside. (TOM KELLY)

Two different hangars as they are today, both of the hangars were built during WW II.
(TOM KELLY)

Williams Gateway Chapel now called Gilbert Family Church. (TOM KELLY)

its various training programs, but the dust and extreme desert heat were causing problems especially in the Link Trainer buildings. The Link trainers were flight simulators used to help teach a student instrument flight. Although primitive by today's standards, they were state of the art in 1942, and they were the forerunners of today's highly complex and expensive flight simulators. They contained many vacuum tubes and electronics that required a dust free environment and moderate temperatures. Unfortunately, this wasn't possible because the buildings that housed them were drafty and had no installation or climate control. To help fix the dust problem, the buildings were insulated and sealed inside with gypsum board. This solved the dust problem, but the lack of circulation caused the students to sweat excessively, so much so that their perspiration caused the headphone and microphone cords to fail. Eventually the building had air coolers installed, which lowered the temperature a little but created high humidity that, in turn, damaged the electronics of the trainers. Later, the buildings would be air-conditioned, a luxury in 1942.

The extreme heat at this dessert-training base created problems that affected everyone, especially the crews of the training aircraft. Maurice (Maurie) Kelly was a B-17 instructor pilot and

recalled that summer training missions often saw the heat climb into the 120-degree range on the ramps, yet regulations required the crews to wear their leather, fleece lined high altitude flying clothes from the very beginning of the flight. To beat the problem, once aboard the plane the crews would immediately begin to remove their heavy clothing. Often, they would take off wearing only their underclothing. As they gained altitude and cooler air the clothes would come back on, and at the end of the flight off they went, until ready to leave the aircraft when they were put back on.

To help control the overall dust problem, improve drainage, and beautify the drab military base filled with temporary wooden structures, a grand design of trees, shrubs, and grass was submitted by the engineer's office in Los Angeles. There wasn't the money available to handle such a complex project, so a more efficient plan was

A painting by the class of 87-01 on the ceiling of one of the Williams buildings. (TOM KELLY)

99

This 1943 view shows the swimming pool that was built by the officers and enlisted men along with civilian help. In the distance are the obstacle course and the Superstition Mountains. (TOM KELLY)

set up locally by Lieutenant Rigler, the officer who had the task of landscaping the post.

He decided to start with the cactus plants that were available locally, and with the help of prisoners, brought in 17 truckloads from the nearby area. At this time, the field was on a seven-day workweek and some soldiers went into the nearby foothills on Sundays to help gather the plants. Using additional prison labor, along with about 50 men from the Works Projects Administration, trees were planted throughout the new post along its many streets. The hot climate and extremely hard soil required dynamite at times to dig the necessary six-foot deep holes. Many different trees were planted including, date palms, mulberry, sour orange, Texas umbrella, and Chinese elm. When the project was completed at the end of 1942, about 14,000 different trees and shrubs were in place along with lots of grass seed.

By the end of 1942, the field had facilities to handle 819 officers, 1,275 cadets, and 6,790 enlisted men. The cost had grown to about 11 million dollars (or about 140 million dollars today).

Construction would continue through 1943, and by the end of that year the field had 461 buildings of all kinds. These included living quarters (for military and civilians), mess halls, administration buildings, classrooms, theatres, a 15 building hospital, nine hangars, and 36 warehouses. At this point, Williams had seven auxiliary fields, one of which was Ajo Field (used for gunnery training) with 110 buildings. Another auxiliary (Coolidge) consisted of 85 buildings.

When news of the bombing of Pearl Harbor reached the field (about 2:00 in the afternoon of December 7th), there was not much in the way of a guard to protect the base. The newly arrived military police were still trying to learn their way around the unfamiliar base. The field was still under construction, there were no roads, lots of dust, no street lights, and the field was littered with construction trenches, which the guards sometimes fell into at night. To protect the base, the guards had a mix of about seven guns that varied from 22 caliber rifles to 12 gauge shot guns. There was no extra ammunition, so a man was sent to nearby Luke Field to borrow

Former living quarters as they are today. (TOM KELLY)

some machine guns, rifles, bayonets, flashlights, and the necessary ammunition. Since the rifles and machine guns were packed in heavy grease, it was necessary to clean and reassemble them before they could be used. At about 2:00 the next morning the guards were ready with their new weapons. One can only imagine what these young men were thinking that night, alone in the middle of a dark construction area, sitting in the desert.

According to the field's history, the first plane to land at Williams was a BT-13A, piloted by Major Bridget who landed on an empty part of the base behind the hospital on October 28, 1941. Actually any number of planes could have landed here before this. It was common practice in those days for a military pilot to land on a field during its construction phase just to claim the record for the first landing. Sometimes they would claim they were "lost" or had engine trouble. Speaking of firsts, another was a mascot, a dog-named "Brucie," owned by Mr. John Lane. The dog delighted in chasing jackrabbits across the airfield much to the amusement of the soldiers on the base. Rattlesnakes were in abundance at the field, but there is no report of Brucie chasing them.

Williams Field was in the center of a beehive of flight instruction because of its proximity to several other USAAF training fields. Nearby at Glendale and Scottsdale (north and west of Williams) were Thunderbird Fields #1 and #2. Here, civilian instructors gave cadets Primary flight instruction. Luke Army Air Field, also north and west of Williams, was located in Litchfield, Arizona and was an Advanced training base. So it was possible for an aviation student in 1942, to progress from Primary through Advanced training all within an area of approximately 40 miles. Luke Field is still an active Air Force installation today.

The year 1942 was an active one for Williams Field. During this time the field held several training and processing activities. The first airmen to train at Williams were Chinese cadets who came to the field in early January 1942. They would be followed by another class and took their Basic Flight training here. The men had come from Thunderbird Field were they had graduated from Primary training. For a brief period of time, Williams was also a Reception Center for Pre-Flight cadets. The first cadets arrived in February, and by the time Williams had filled its role as a reception center at the end of February, a total of 1,920 cadets passed through its gates. At the end of February, cadets arrived to take Advanced training (Class 42 D) at the field. These would be the first American cadets to take flight training at Williams. A total of 1,044 pilots were graduated in 1942.

While this activity was in progress, a school for Bombardier training was started in June 1942. There were 403 Bombardier Cadets graduated that year. The remainder would finish in 1943. After that, the field would settle down to training only pilots. So in 1942, the first year of operation for the new training base, Williams was used for Basic flight training, a Reception Center, Advanced Training, and Bombardier Training. This rather complex and varied mix of activity was a good reflection of the state our readiness in 1942; the situation was desperate. As a result, many stop gap measures were necessary to make up for the time lost because of our government's failure to adequately maintain our military forces. Unfortunately, many young men would pay with their lives for this failure.

The activity for which Williams Field became known during World War II was the training of twin engine pilots. While other training took place at the field, the twin engine training was the most important, and would ultimately result in turning out thousands of P-38 pilots. Actually, the training of the first American cadets started with the single engine AT-6 (Texan) in February 1942. This was the only advanced training aircraft on the field at the time. In addition to the Texans already in use, the AT-9 began arriving in late February. This plane (nicknamed the "Jeep") was a twin engine trainer built by Curtiss. Over time, the plane would gain the reputation of being too difficult for low time students to fly; however, by late 1943, there were 167 assigned to the Field. (As a side note, at war's end when the government was selling thousands of military surplus aircraft, the AT-9 was not put on the market because it was felt the "Jeep" was too demanding for the average private pilot.) By March there were 18 "Jeeps" on the base and the

training was divided into single engine advanced and twin engine advanced.

Another aircraft used for advanced twin engine training at the time was the Beech AT –10 "Wichita." This aircraft also has an interesting history because of the material used in its construction. This ship was built almost entirely of wood and was the first all wood aircraft to be accepted by the USAAF as an advanced trainer. The plane even had wooden fuel tanks lined with a special synthetic rubber. Because of its wooden construction, furniture manufacturers and other woodworking companies were able to build major sub-assemblies.

The all-wood construction of the AT-10 would prove deadly to the aspiring pilots at Williams. There were 79 "Wichita's" assigned

This T-38 was sitting on a pylon during the time Williams Air Force Base was active and is now waiting its fate. Note the 82nd Flying Training Wing markings on the tail. (TOM KELLY)

Here's a survivor from the WW II days of Williams Field. (TOM KELLY)

taled at least 348, including 237 T-6s. The average amount of gasoline being used at this time was about 1,025,000 gallons per month.

Early 1944 saw flight training at Williams basically the same as late 1943, with the aircraft in use being the AT-6, AT-9, and the RP-322 (a version of the P-38 Lightning). All the flight trainees received training in the AT-6, and some selected men were then given additional instruction using the AT-9. After finishing this phase they moved on to the RP-322. There were 438 aircraft assigned to the field, including 349 AT-6s. The number of deaths due to training accidents had grown to 31.

Today, when just the mention of God is being eliminated from our schools and public buildings, it's refreshing to note the emphasis on faith by the students of Williams Field. Among other things, the official base history reports, "A new tradition found its way into the Catholic activities at the suggestion of Cadet Class 44-B. The Catholic cadets of that class had a Mass of Thanksgiving on the day of their graduation, at which they all received Holy Communion in a body."

By early 1944, hundreds of aircrew training facilities across the United States were in full swing and graduating huge numbers of trained men. As an example, Williams Field graduated its largest pilot class in March (Class 44-C) which totaled 531 pilots. With the desperate need for some types of trained aircrew being met, there was now the extra time to extend the training and be more thorough.

One direct result of the growing number of trained pilots was the extension of the four pilot training phases (Preflight, Primary, Basic, and Advanced) from 9 to 10 weeks. This increased training began at Williams Field with Class 44-E on March 14. At the same, time there was the continuing surplus of men awaiting training. As one measure to help address the problem, the Training Command decided to send these men to the various training fields on a temporary basis and called the program "on-the-line training." The program is described in the series *The Army Air Forces In World War II* as having two objectives: "to provide storage and training of delayed students and to alleviate the growing shortage

to the field in July 1942, during which time, three cadets were killed in the crashes of two AT-10s. All were members of Class 42 H. The accidents resulted from structural failures caused by the hot, dry climate drying out the wood and glue of the planes. Training with the AT-10 was stopped and the planes shipped to areas with higher humidity where they served well. In total, 10 aviation cadets lost their lives in training during 1942 at Williams Field.

By January 1943 there were about 176 aircraft assigned to Williams Field, the most numerous being the AT-9 and the AT-17. The AT-17 ("Bobcat") was a twin engine advanced trainer built by Cessna. Thought by some at Williams as too easy to fly, it was phased out during 1943 for the more difficult AT-9.

The number of aircraft at Williams grew rapidly as the training increased, and this is reflected in the report of gasoline dispatched by the refueling department. In 1943 the number of aircraft to-

1,178 civilian employees. Continued effort was put into improving the entertainment facilities of the field, one aspect of which was the building of a beer garden. The new facility was called "Willie's Beer Hanger," and was opened on March 22, 1944 with a dedication speech by the base commanding officer Col. Herbert Grills. Free beer, sandwiches, potato chips, and popcorn were served to the more than 1000 who attended. The beer garden was next to the main Post Exchange, and was built in a half moon shape with a bar that was sixty feet long.

Over the course of Williams Field's early history, there were many changes in its flight training programs and in the types of training given by the school. By May 1944, the flying school

of regularly assigned personnel at the airfields." Each field was given a wide latitude on how to utilize these men and what training they were to receive. In most cases, they replaced personnel on the flight lines doing simple maintenance chores; later some would be used for administrative and non-technical duties. Williams Field received 250 "on-the-line" trainees on February 10, 1944. They were assigned to the flight line for at least six hours of on the job training in maintenance and servicing aircraft, in addition to some time spent on physical training, and classroom work. When the Air Forces college training program was stopped, additional men who had been in the program were sent to various bases. Williams received 930 of these men from schools such as Texas Technical College, Morningside College, Knox College, Illinois State Teachers College and Drake University. Their day started at 5:00 AM with reveille and ended at 10:00 with lights out.

The number of military personnel assigned to Williams Field in April 1944 totaled 5,724 (including those assigned to Ajo AAF). Working alongside of the military personnel at the two fields were

The Compass Rose slowly being obscured by weeds. (TOM KELLY)

A partial view of the former base housing area. The homes are sitting derelict awaiting sale or destruction. The photo was taken in 1999. (TOM KELLY)

was involved in four courses of instruction. By far the largest flight program was the single engine advanced course where students received advanced training in the AT-6. Other students received twin engine training in the AT-9 and then on the RP-322. This training was intended to prepare pilots for photo reconnaissance missions. Another course of instruction was that given to small numbers of men who had already received their wings and were assigned to the field for twin engine fighter transition, also in the RP-322. The official history reports that "during 1943 and a part of 1944, Williams Field was unique in that it was the only P-38 Transition School in the country." The last type of training was a one-month program given to newly assigned instructors. During July and August another flying program in progress was the night fighter-training program. These students received additional navigation training and took their gunnery training at Ajo Army Air Field.

A major change in the training mission at Williams Field was in the works towards the end of 1944. Late in 1944, the new pilot training classes entering the training center were becoming smaller because new pilot training was being cut on a nation wide basis. At this point (late 1944) there was an ample supply of pilots in training. Craven and Cate in their history *The Army Air Forces In World War II* note "the peak

was reached in December 1943 when over 74,000 students were in the various stages of individual pilot training." As a result, classes entering Williams were reduced in 1944. By late 1944, the field was told to discontinue single engine training in the T-6. The field was also instructed to begin preparations for B-17 Transition Training. So with Single Engine Training being discontinued work began on the new training mission, during which time the last Single Engine Advanced class graduated (Class 44-J) on December 23, 1944.

The Advanced Pilot training program had run from February 1942 until the last class graduated on December 23, 1944. During that time, the field's personnel had trained and graduated 8,490 pilots. Not included in this number are the graduates (Chinese and American) Basic and Advanced trainees, and the men who received Bombardier training. This is an impressive number, and a magnificent achievement by anyone's standards.

The training center officially became a Four-Engine Transitional Training Field on December 10, 1944, and the pilot school was renamed Army Air Forces Pilot School (Specialized Four-Engine). Its students would be officers and flight officers who had already earned their wings. At the end of December, most of the AT-6s had shipped out of the field and in their place were

53 B-17s; just three months later there were just four AT-6s and 76 B-17s. At this time the field was well into the B-17 pilot transition program.

Some of the more interesting training was three engine running take-offs, two engine landings, and landing with no flaps. These procedures were practiced in daylight only to insure maximum safety. Also of interest were the crosswind take-offs and landings in crosswinds up to 15 miles per hour. About one third of the training was accomplished at night.

Lt. Maurice Kelly, was a B-17 instructor pilot and instrument check pilot at Williams Field for a short time (November 1944–March 1945) and would go on to fly over 2,000 hours in the B-17. Later Maurie would command many other types of aircraft including the B-29 and the massive B-36. Tom Kelly followed his Dad's footsteps earning his commercial pilot's license with instrument, and multi-engine ratings.

Tom and his dad shared many pleasant hours flying a variety of aircraft together until Maurice's death at the age of 80 in 2000. Tom still recalls some of the anecdotes his father told him about his time as an instructor at Willie. One story concerns B-17 training flights that often took the aircraft west from Williams to an area near Luke Field, which at the time, had some pilots flying the P-40. Fighter pilots love to make mock attacks on other aircraft and especially love to show up pilots who flew the slow lumbering bombers. Not to be outdone by the Luke pilots, Maurie would delight in impressing the aggressive fighter pilots by throwing his lightly loaded and stripped B-17 through the air when jumped by the P-40s.

Tom's dad also had a unique way to celebrate Tom's birth. What better way to celebrate than to buzz the family farm, then cap it off by flying his B-17 down the main street of the small nearby town of Schuyler, Nebraska? This he did, and while doing so, managed to fly below the town's water tower to the cheering of the folks of Schuyler. Buzzing was a serious offense and often resulted in disciplinary action against the pilot. Perhaps then Lt. Kelly did not worry about it because the godfather of his new son would be the commanding officer of Williams Field, Col. Grills.

The training of B-17 pilots began in late December 1944 and ended in April 1945, graduating 608 officers for the B-17 program.

Another brief, but important program starting in April 1945 was the training of radar operators on bombing and navigational techniques using the then secret APQ-7 radar and the confidential APQ-13 radar. The school was called the Radar Observers School and the planes used for this training were the B-25 and B-24. At the end of July, there were forty-three B-25s and eighty-four B-24s assigned to Williams Field for use in the training of radar observers. That was the peak of radar training at Williams Field with a total of 418 students were in training.

During 1945, Williams Field had three different base commanders. They were, Col. Herbert Grills, who replaced the field's

Lt. Maurice Kelly holding his infant son Tom.
(TOM KELLY)

first commanding officer, Col. Albert Woody, and Col. Roy Osborn. The field's first commanding officer, Col. Bernard Bridget who served as the CO of the field to March 1943, would go on to earn the Bronze Star in the Central Pacific in operations against the Japanese.

When the war ended, Williams was involved in turning out qualified radar operators, and at the time, 709 officer students had graduated. The training stopped for a couple of days but then resumed, but at a much reduced rate. Clearly the focus of Williams Field had changed, as expressed by the then commanding officer Col. Albert Woody. He mentioned in a meeting on August 27, 1945, that the mission of the post was (1) feeding the men, (2) processing records, (3) expedience of getting men out promptly on orders, and (4) training.

After World War II, most of the temporary training bases were put on inactive status and eventually closed. This was particularly true for bases like Williams that had sprung up overnight and were built with mostly wooden temporary type structures. Williams would be an exception in not closing, but over the years expanding into a premier Air Force training base. The field continued to train highly qualified personnel who went on to serve their country with distinction. It's interesting to note that when the base finally closed in 1994, the two men who as Boy Scouts had raised the flag at its opening over fifty years be-

The first and last graduates of Williams Air Force Base. Shown are Mr. Clark Smith class of 1942 and 2nd Lt. Corey Wormack class of 1993.
(MESA SOUTHWEST MUSEUM)

fore, were there to lower the flag at the closing.

Today Williams Field continues to serve the Phoenix area as a growing industrial park and as a first-class aviation facility.

The main gate at Columbus AFB. Note the T-38 on the left and the T-37 on the right of the road. Since 9/11 additional security has been put into place around the gate.

(CONNIE LISOWSKI, 14TH FLYING TRAINING WING, HISTORY OFFICE)

8

The World's Finest Military Pilots

COLUMBUS AIR FORCE BASE

Sitting on the outskirts of the rural community of Columbus, Mississippi is one of the best-kept secrets of the United States Air Force. Here, among the pines of north east Mississippi located near the Alabama border on 6,015 acres, the 14th Flying Training Wing goes about its job of producing the world's finest military pilots.

The birthday of Columbus Air Force Base was June 26, 1941, the date when the War Department (Department of Defense) approved the site for construction. At that time, most of the land was leased to the government for 99 years for $1.00 a year by the city of Columbus, Mississippi and Lowndes County. Soon after, on September 12, 1941, construction work on what was then called the "Advanced Twin Engine Flying School" started. By then the preliminary work had been completed and construction of the runways and cantonment area began. Eventually there would be four 150' wide, 4,500' long runways and seven auxiliary landing fields. The landing strips, taxi ways and ramp areas covered a large part of the field's initial 4,268 acres.

The field's first commanding officer, Col. Louie C. Mallory, was also its project officer during the construction of the new training base. Colonel Mallory began his duties as project officer on July 18, 1941. He would serve in this capacity and later as the commanding officer of the field until April 5, 1945. Col. Mallory arrived at the site when it was just open fields, directed the construction of the new training center, and then managed the training of thousands of fledgling pilots through most of World War II.

Pilot training at the newly built advanced twin engine base began on February 9, 1942. It was then called Kaye Field. The field was named after Captain Sam Kaye who served with distinction in World War I as a member of the famed 94th "Hat-in-the-Ring" squadron commanded by Eddie Rickenbacker. Captain Kaye earned several decorations for bravery including the Distinguished Service Cross and the Croix de Guerre. Captain Kaye was a native of Columbus, Mississippi.

The first class to graduate from the new training center was class 42-C, which graduated on March 6, 1942. It was at this time the name of the field was changed to avoid confusion with another training field, Key Field in Meridian,

Aerial View of the base as it was in 1945. Note the four runways and the wide expanse of ramp.
(SS KYLE FORD, 14TH FLYING TRAINING WING PA OFFICE)

A recent photo of Columbus AFB. There are three parallel runways, the longest 12,000 feet long.
(CONNIE LISOWSKI, 14TH FLYING TRAINING WING, HISTORY OFFICE)

Above: Headquarters building for the 14th Flying Training Wing. Left: Part of the memorial that stands in front of the 14th Flying Training Wing Headquarters. The inscription reads: "The monument is dedicated to Columbus Air Force Base pilot training graduates and students who placed nation above self and made the ultimate sacrifice in the service of their country."

Mississippi. The new name was Columbus Army Flying School; later this was changed to Columbus Army Air Field.

Regardless of its name, the new training center began its mission of turning out highly competent twin engine pilots. A good example of this, and an indication of what set Columbus Army Air Field apart from so many other training fields, is the story of Lt. Col. Joseph Duckworth, director of training at the field at the time.

As director of training, the Colonel became aware that many young pilots had a poor knowledge of and ability to fly an aircraft in instrument weather conditions. One of the more important reasons for the lack of instrument flying skills was time. The desperate need for pilots had caused the total instructional time for flight training to be cut from twelve months in early 1939 to just seven months in May 1940. As a side note, one of the problems reported by the B-24 training personnel at Smyrna Army Air Field, Smyrna, Tennessee at this time was the lack of instrument skills demonstrated by many of the already rated commercial pilots being trained at the base.

Unfortunately, the military pilot did not have the luxury to avoid flying in bad weather but flew when and where the mission

Part view of the ramp showing some of the T-38s and T-37s assigned to the base.

Class has just finished and some students are making final notes prior to leaving.

Above: Some of the training aids used in class. This particular class was on advanced navigation. Right: The curriculum is tough and demanding. Here a student is using a bit of free time (lunch) to review his flight plan for the afternoon's flight.

required. Some pilots were losing their lives because of their lack of ability to fly in instrument conditions.

So Col. Duckworth set about to improve the instrument training at Columbus Army Air Field using his knowledge and experience—over 12,000 flying hours with Eastern Airlines. The Navy had developed a better method of instrument flying in 1942 and this had been observed by some Army Air Forces instructors. Colonel Duckworth changed the existing course at Co-

lumbus Army Air Field. The course taught the student to use just three basic flight instruments (rate of turn, bank indicator, and airspeed indicator). He changed it to a program of instruction that required the student to become proficient not only in the basic three, but several more, including the artificial horizon and the directional gyroscope. As a result, the fledging pilot had a much clearer picture of the plane's flight performance and progress over the ground during poor weather conditions.

The results were clear and immediate. So much so, that Gen. "Hap" Arnold, head of the Army Air Forces, and Maj. Gen. Barton Yount, who commanded the Army Air Forces Flying Training Command, visited the field to see the program. Eventually, the new system became standard throughout the Air Forces. The new training course was so successful that it received coverage in two national publications.

The training center continued to turn out pilots until its last training class graduated on May 23, 1945. Col. Mallory, the former base commander, was there as a guest speaker and proud witness to the impressive training record of his base. During his tenure as commanding officer and until training stopped at Columbus Army Air Field, 7,412 students successfully completed the rigorous training program and earned their wings. The base set an impressive safety record during this time. The students flew 181,000 hours, or about 24 million miles, without a fatal accident. This was thought to be a world record for flying safety and represented an accident rate of 50% less than the average for the entire Training Command. To put this accomplishment into better perspective, 181,000 hours is equal to 22,625 eight-hour days, or almost 62 years of eight-hour days. Even so, 31 students lost their lives in training, part of the almost 15,000 young men who were killed in aircrew training accidents in the Army Air Forces during World War II.

With the end of World War II, training slowed, and eventually the base was shut down. Just a

Interior view of the maintenance hangar for the 80 T-38s and 90 T-37s used in training. Note the immaculate condition of the facility.

Two views of the "mole hole" the former Alert Facility for the SAC pilots and crew. The ramps lead to the lower level of the facility where the crew had sleeping and living accommodations.

few people remained behind to help maintain the facilities. This period of inactivity did not last long; however, as the Korean War saw the base reactivated as a civilian contracted training facility in 1951. At this point, the field was called Columbus Air Force Base. The base was used to train pilots to fly the T-6 Texan. By 1953, with training in full swing, there were 125 T-6s assigned to the base. The base continued to train pilots until March 1955 when the last class graduated. During this part of the base's history, about 3,000 pilots were trained, some of whom were students from foreign countries. The last class graduated in March 1955, and in April the base became part of the Strategic Air Command (SAC).

Without question, the Strategic Air Command played a major role (some would say the key role) in preventing a world war during its forty-six years of existence. Their motto "Peace Is Our Profession" was backed by the finest, most demanding, aerial organization the world has ever seen. To be in SAC was to be among the elite of the Air Force. Columbus Air Force Base was selected to become part of that team in April 1955. To help prepare the base for its new mission, a major facility upgrade was required. These improvements included, refurbishing and adding to an existing runway, and the building of a major base housing project. Over

time, there were 15 B-52s, and 15 KC-135s assigned to the base.

The 454th Bomb Wing, stationed at Columbus Air Force Base during this period, added to the tradition of excellence that had long been part of the base history. In September 1965, the 736 Bombardment Squadron (Crew S-02) won the annual Bombing-Navigation Competition, and as a result, was awarded the Fairchild Trophy. This is the "Super Bowl" of SAC, and is the ultimate compliment to a crew that earns it by competing with the best of the best. The unit also flew combat missions over Vietnam and was deployed on three separate occasions. The 454th Bomb Wing was awarded the Air Force Outstanding Unit Award for two of its deployments.

Another change was in store for Columbus Air Force base because by the late 1960s the need for SAC bases had been reduced. So after 14 years in SAC, the base found itself preparing to return to the training business. There are still reminders that remain on the base of the former presence of SAC and the part Columbus Air Force base played during the Cold War. One of the more visible is the "mole hole." This is the facility where the SAC alert crews would live while awaiting a call to get their bombers and tankers into the air for a practice mission or to make a nuclear strike.

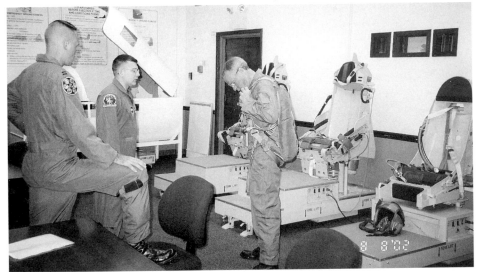

Here the author is being checked out in the proper wearing of the parachute. Behind him are ejection seat trainers, and to his right in the far corner is the device for training in T-37 emergency ground egress. Observing are SS Brent Ochs and Captain Timothy Sundvall. (DAVE)

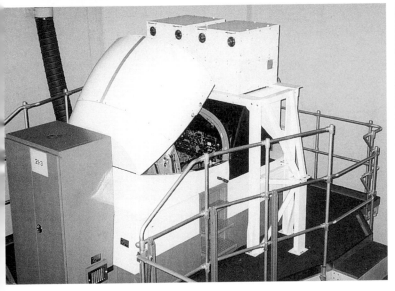

An exterior view of the T-37 simulator. A partial view of the instrument panel of the T-37 B. The student normally sits in the left-hand seat, the instructor in the right.

After the phase out of SAC at Columbus, pilot training began again on July 17, 1969. This time instead of propeller driven twin engine trainers (WW II) or single engine trainers (Korea), the new trainers were twin engine jets. There were two types, the basic trainer T-37 B (Tweet) and the supersonic trainer, the T-38 (Talon). In order to accommodate the higher landing speeds of the T-38, a longer runway was built.

Columbus AFB has three parallel runways, each with a specific name and purpose. The center runway is 12,000' long and 300' wide and is used for visiting aircraft and instrument training. It is also a back up landing strip for the space shuttle when it is ferried back to Cape Canaveral after land-

This is a 1943 look at two Link Trainers at Columbus Army Air Field. These were the instrument trainers used in WW II pilot training and a forerunner of today's highly complex flight simulators.
(CONNIE LISOWSKI, 14TH FLYING TRAINING WING HISTORY OFFICE.)

A formation take off as photographed by the author from the accompanying T-37 flown by Captain Timothy Sundvall.

ing in California. Another runway is 8,000' long and 150' wide and is the main runway for the T-38 and T-1 (a Lear Jet type trainer). The third runway, 6,000' long and 175' wide, is used mostly for the T-37. To compare runways from a World War II training base with this is somewhat difficult. Often runway lengths varied depending upon the mission of the field; however, the majority of World War II training base runways were about 5,500' long and 150' wide.

To gain some insight into the SUPT (Specialized Undergraduate Pilot Training) program of today's Air Force, I was privileged to spend two days at Columbus Air Force Base in August, 2002 as a guest of Colonel Thomas Quelly and the 14th Flying Training Wing. The wing, whose motto is "Day and Night—Peace and War," has been turning out pilots here since 1972.

This view shows the underside of the T-37 B as the author's plane slides underneath.

Their mission is "To Defend the United States of America by Building the World's Best Pilots, Leaders, and Warriors."

The lineage of the 14th Flying Training Wing is long and proud. It began as the 14th Fighter

A nice view of the T-37 B as seen during the formation take off. The planes have just entered the initial turn. Student pilots are taught to fly within three feet of the formation plane's wing tip.

Wing in July 1947, and its first major assignment was to provide air defense for the northeastern United States. Later the wing, redesignated the 14th Special Operations Wing, would see combat in Southeast Asia, (1966–1971) and operate Nha Trang AB. The wing's personnel also trained South Vietnamese Air Force personnel in the use and maintenance of the AC-119 gun ship. Today the wing runs the SUPT program at Columbus Air Force Base. The base has a workforce of 1,410 military personnel (including student pilots) and 1,267 civilian employees.

Today the Air Force has just three pilot training bases. One of these is Columbus AFB, the other two are located at Laughlin AFB, in Del Rio, Texas and Vance AFB, in Enid, Oklahoma. There is some pilot training done at other bases, but the majority of the new pilots are trained at Columbus, Laughlin and Vance.

The training track for the hopeful Air Force pilot starts long before he or she arrives at the gate at Columbus Air Force base. By this time the fledging pilot will have earned his private pilot's license flying either a Cessna 152 or a Cessna 172 under the tutelage of a private contractor licensed by the Air Force. This initial phase of the program is designed to help insure the potential pilot has the basic skills necessary to successfully complete the Air Force pilot training. The pilot trainees are officers, most are second lieutenants, and come from the Air Force, the Air Force Reserves, the Air National Guard, or the Air Force Academy. The welcome letter they receive from the commander of the 14th Flying Training Wing makes clear why they are here. It reads in part: "You are beginning a year of intense training that will culminate with your being awarded wings-provided you remain committed to the task. ... Upon arrival at Columbus AFB, be physically and mentally prepared for the most exciting and challenging 52 weeks of your life."

The route into pilot training was quite different during WW II. Then the Air Force was not a separate branch of service but part of the Army and called the United States Army Air Forces. Only men were allowed to apply, and early on were required to have two years college education. Virtually all came directly from civilian ranks, and it was a time of explosive growth. From January 1, 1942 (less than a month after Pearl Harbor) to June 30, 1943, the Army Air Forces grew from 354,161 to 2,197,114 men and women. At this time, (March 1944) flying training consisted of Preflight, Primary, Basic, Advanced, and Transition. Each course was 10 weeks long. The exception was Transition training for fighter pilots, which was five weeks and included gunnery training.

In a tradition that goes back to WW II training, each class has a "dunking pool" that the students are thrown into following first solo. Each class decorates the "pool" with their own design.

For comparison purposes, I will contrast the USAAF pilot training program as it was in 1944 with that of today's (2002) pilot training program. In 1944, the United States had been at war for about two and a half years, and by then aircrew training had evolved from a rushed, make do program to a more structured, formalized training process. To get to this point, the USAAF took unprecedented steps to meet the need for trained aircrew members and technicians. One of the many steps taken to meet its training goals was to lease 68 civilian mechanics schools to help train technicians. The Air Forces also purchased or leased 452 hotels and converted them into schools and barracks. In addition, to meet the training needs of aircrew members and others, there were 345 major Air Force bases, 116 smaller bases, and 322 auxiliary landing fields. To help with the gunnery and bombing training, there were 480 gunnery and bombing areas that covered millions of acres. Today there are 82 major Air Force installations worldwide.

Pilot training in World War II was a fluid and constantly changing program that was based upon the needs of the time. For example, in July 1939 total training time was cut from twelve to nine months. Then in May 1940, the time was cut again to seven months. Still later, shortly after Pearl Harbor, the time allocated to primary, basic and advanced training was cut again from ten weeks to nine weeks. After the desperate need for pilots had been met, the training time allocated for each stage was increased to ten weeks in March, 1944.

Today's pilot training is called Specialized Undergraduate Pilot Training or SUPT. This is the training program conducted at Columbus Air Force Base, the successful completion of which earns the pilot his or her coveted Silver Wings. There are three parts to SUPT, Phase I, Phase II and Phase III. Following graduation, the pilots receive further specialized training at other bases.

The Phase I training, covering strictly academics, is four weeks long. Phase I can be compared with the Preflight phase of the WW II program. In each case it is academics and no flying. Preflight was a 10-week course.

The intent of Phase I is to introduce the student to flying fundamentals and the basic operation of the T-37 systems. One of the study guides the student receives during this period is the flight manual for the T-37, called the "Dash One" for short. The Dash One has about 116 double sided pages; much of it must be committed to memory. The manual covers the aircraft, its systems, operating limitations, emergency procedures, instruments, and the many graphs and charts necessary to plan a safe flight. To the uninformed, the flight manual appears highly complex, and it is, yet the T-37 is the most simple and forgiving aircraft the students will fly in the SUPT program.

Unlike civilian schools where the completion of study assignments is often left to choice, in SUPT study assignments are considered direct orders. Students who fail a test are required to retake the examination within five working days. If the student fails three academic examinations, the Squadron Commander recommends him or her for elimination from the program.

Additional subjects taught in Phase I include aerodynamics, use of basic navigation instruments, and instruction on emergency procedures. Much of the emergency training is accomplished at the Aerospace Physiology complex, which has an ejection seat trainer, a mock up of the T-37 fuselage (for ground egress emergency training) and an altitude chamber. While at the Aerospace Physiology Center, the student learns how the flying environment affects the body, how to take care of and tell if something is wrong with the equipment, parachuting procedures, egress procedures, survival techniques for the local area and ground training. Part of this training includes time in the altitude chamber where the student learns about the effect of hypoxia (lack of oxygen). One of the more fun parts of the training is para-sailing where the student learns proper parachute handling techniques. While at the Aerospace Physiology Center, the student is fitted with the proper emergency gear. This includes the flight helmet, which is custom fitted. In total, eight and a half days are spent at the Center during Phase I.

The T-37 is designed to insure the student pilot receives a solid foundation in basic flying skills, which includes instrument flying, aerobatics, and formation flying. It was manufactured by the Cessna Aircraft Company and features side by side seating, ejection seats, full instrumentation, and air conditioning. Its wingspan is about 34 feet and fully loaded weighs 7,000 lbs. With a speed range of 85 to 425 mph, it's an efficient trainer, and has been in service since 1957. Student pilots affectionately refer to the Tweet as a wonderfully efficient machine for converting jet fuel to noise.

While the T-37 is a simple aircraft in rela-

tion to the other planes in the Air Force inventory, nothing is left to chance, especially in the area of flight safety. The emergency egress system that includes an ejection seat, has been proven many times over in emergency bailouts, always bringing its occupant down safely.

Strapping on a T-37 for the first time can be a confusing and perplexing experience. Even after having rehearsed the procedure twice in the prior safety briefings, I still found it somewhat intimidating. Getting into the aircraft is easy, and once seated the fun begins. The pilot is now faced with several hoses, wires, belts, and safety equipment that must be properly arranged and connected. Thankfully, the crew chief is right outside the canopy to make sure things are set as required. Just before engine start-up, the pilot makes his own safety check.

You truly begin to feel you are part of the aircraft as your communication system wires (leading from your oxygen mask) are plugged into the proper cockpit receptacles. Meanwhile, the oxygen hose from the facemask has to be connected, first to a receptacle on the parachute harness, and then to the aircraft. The reason for

The author and his son, Major David Thole prior to the T-37 flight. (SUNDVALL)

119

the receptacle on the parachute harness is that the parachute pack contains a self contained oxygen system that supplies oxygen to the wearer, should it be needed for bailout over 10,000'. By this time, the various safety belts have been hooked up securing the wearer to the plane. One of the more important ones is the Zero Delay Lanyard, which helps to insure proper seat operation at altitudes below 10,000'. Ejection from the ship is quite simple; just assume the proper seat position, lift the handgrips, squeeze the triggers and you're out. Within 2.9 seconds the parachute pack opens. All of this assumes you have removed the safety pin from the arming system of the seat prior to the flight. This is assured by removing the pin, attached to a large "Remove Before Flight" flag and shown to the crew chief standing on the ground. The timing and operation of the seat will vary according to altitude, attitude, and speed. Once past 10,000 feet additional safety checks are made, one of which is to insure proper oxygen flow. The cockpit of the T-37 is not pressurized, so flight is normally restricted to altitudes below 18,000'.

Sitting on the tarmac on a hot, muggy August day waiting for the clearance to taxi, the thought seeps into your mind that this is not all fun and games. It can be hard, demanding, and sometimes dangerous work. The sweat begins to run from your face and along the edges of your oxygen mask, and you're anxious for the canopy to be closed and the air conditioning to cool the cockpit.

The successful completion of Phase I allows the student pilot to begin Phase II, a five-month program. Here's where the student begins his or her Air Force flying with the T-37. Prior to this time, the only sanctioned military flying has been with the Cessna 152 or Cessna 172, which, as mentioned, is a screening exercise. This training is not done at Columbus AFB but at another location, typically a civilian airport, near an Air Force base. The instructor is a civilian under contract to the Air Force. During this part of the process, the hopeful pilot is considered on "casual status" and assigned to a nearby Air Force Base. The primary duty is to earn a pri-

vate pilot license. This part of the training is called Introductory Flight Training.

The Phase II portion of SUPT is similar to the Primary and Basic phase of World War II pilot training. It was in the Primary and Basic pilot training that the airmen of WW II flew his first military aircraft. During Primary, he flew 70 hours in a single engine open cockpit biplane or a low-wing monoplane. Often this was the Stearman PT-17, a very forgiving aircraft, but with a nasty tendency to ground loop because of its narrow wheelbase. This aircraft had a 220 HP radial engine with a top speed of about 120 miles an hour. A simple, rugged aircraft, it had only basic flight instruments, no radio, and tandem seating. It was fully aerobatic. There were about 3,520 produced during WW II. The airplane is a classic, and many are still flown today. Other Primary Trainers included the Fairchild PT-19 and Ryan PT-22. These were low-wing monoplanes with tandem seating. Students and instructors favored the PT-17, although over 5,600 PT-19 and PT-22s were built.

After the WW II pilot cadet finished Primary Training he went on to Basic Flight Training. Here among other subjects he was taught to fly either the BT-13 or BT-15. He received about 70 hours in the aircraft along with ground school and military training. The Vultee Aircraft Company built both the BT-13 and BT-15. They were referred to as the "Vultee Vibrator" because of the rattling noise made by the plane's canopy during a dive. Over 11,500 copies of all models were made. This was a much more complex aircraft than the primary trainer. It was a low wing aircraft with fixed gear, full instrumentation, radios, and a 450-hp engine. Of all the subjects taught during this training phase the most important was instrument training. Here the cadet learned to fly the plane in all weather conditions and at night.

When today's SUPT student moves into Phase II training, he/she will learn to fly the T-37 with the confidence born of thorough training and practice. Phase II training is broken down into four parts, contact, instrument, navigation and formation. The student will receive about 89 hours in this part of the training and will proceed from the most basic steps of how to take off and land to the extremely difficult phase of formation flying. Typically, the student will solo after about 19.5 hours of flight time. Some may take longer and if so, they are required to have soloed before 22 hours.

Important to the flying training is the hours spent in the simulator. Initially the student will spend several hours sitting in front of a non-functioning mock up of the T-37 instrument panel memorizing the location and works of the many dials, buttons, switches, gauges, and levers of the panel. Later they move on to a functioning simulator. While the simulator is somewhat dated, it still is realistic enough to give the feel and challenge of flight in a T-37.

The simulator is fitted out exactly like the cockpit of the T-37. The student enters the simulator along with the instructor, closes the canopy, straps himself into the seat and sits facing the instrument panel and windscreen. The screen is blank. When the instructor starts the machine, the windscreen gives a picture of the tarmac or whatever situation the instructor chooses to program into the simulator's computer. This can be anything from fog, to clear air, calm, or stormy weather. He will also make certain the student has learned his emergency procedures. The simulator can be programmed to have an engine failure, fire, instrument malfunction or any sort of problem that may be faced by the student in actual flight. Additionally, the simulator moves with the student's stick input, so after a while, the student forgets he/she is in a simulator.

One of the more important uses for the simulator is to teach the student how to fly and navigate on instruments without reference to the ground. The use of the simulator for this purpose considerably speeds up the training process and has certainly saved many lives in the process. When a student gets lost flying the simulator or allows the aircraft to get out of control, the only casualty is the student's pride. The simulator screen goes blank and the student tries again.

The World War II pilot also trained on the simulator, if and when they were available. It was called the Link Trainer and designed to teach

a student to fly on instruments. The machine looked like a small carnival type airplane where the student would sit with a basic instrument panel in front of him and under a closed hood. There was no windscreen, and all the student could see was the instrument panel. He was given instructions on what altitude and direction to fly, by an instructor sitting outside the box like structure. The student's progress in following the instructor's instructions was recorded by an instrument on the instructor's desk. While primitive compared with today's simulators, the Link Trainer was extremely effective in teaching students how to fly by instruments.

Learning to fly formation with another T-37 is part of the latter portion of Phase II training. Here the student brings together all the skills learned in the first three parts (contact flying, instrument flying, and navigation) to execute the precise movements necessary to successfully fly in formation. The students are required to fly within 3 feet of wingtip spacing through 90 degrees of bank, and while pulling up to 3 g's. After practice with an instructor, they will do these maneuvers solo. At the end of Phase II, the fledging pilot will have about 89 hours flying time in the T-37.

All is not flying; however, Phase II is also loaded with academics. Typically, the student will spend a half-day in classroom subjects and the remainder in simulator work, flying solo, or flying with an instructor. There are about 350 instructor pilots at Columbus Air Force Base, many of whom are reservists. Typically, each instructor is assigned two to three students for whom he/she is responsible primarily for the paper work and other administrative detail. The student will see 20 to 30 different instructors during his or her journey through SUPT.

There are many similarities to WW II pilot training with the SUPT program of today. There are also major differences, one of them is the manner that the student is treated. The WW II pilot trainee came from many different sources, and very few were officers. More typically the men had no prior military training. As a result, they were subject to endless marching, various drills and intense physical training. They slept

The author and Captain Timothy Sundvall following the orientation flight in the T-37 flown by Captain Sundvall. (DAVE)

in uncomfortable open bay barracks and every minute of their duty day was regimented. Because they were delighted to be receiving flight training, they put up with the harassment, the endless inspections, and the punishment for the least infraction.

Today it's different. The students are commissioned officers (mostly 2nd Lieutenants) typically from the Air Force, the Air Force Reserves, the Air National Guard, or from the Air Force Academy. They have received their basic military training, and are able to focus their energies on becoming pilots. There are no early morning formations, regimented physical training, dormitory conditions, constant inspections, or harassment. Instead they are treated as officers and expected to behave as such. That is not to say their life is not regimented; it is. Any deviation from the 33-page "Student Pilot Handbook" (issued via computer) is met with varying degrees of discipline, from a verbal reprimand to dismissal from the program. Honor, integrity, and personal responsibility are stressed.

The student's Chain of Command starts with his/her Class Leader who is responsible for the activity of the students in the class. The next step in the chain is the Flight Commander, normally the senior ranking officer and a member of the class. The Class Leader represents the class at all functions and works with the Flight Commander. From here the chain progresses through several levels to the Wing Commander. Students are expected to arrive for all scheduled functions at least 5 minutes prior to start time. Of interest is the protocol for briefings. The handbook is very clear on this point: "you will not be late."

I was privileged to interview several students during my visit to Columbus AFB. One of the students, 2nd Lt. Ryan Venhuizen, class 03-07, is a graduate of the ROTC program at the University of Michigan and was in the final weeks of Phase II. Lt. Venhuizen recalls: "I wanted to be a pilot since I was young, and the flying I have done here has been more fun than anything I have ever done. The most enjoyable part has been the solo and formation flying. Right now I can't wait to make my first solo formation flight, I wouldn't change a thing." Lt. Venhuizen who hopes to be assigned to fighter pilot training after he completes Phase II, was "pleasantly surprised by the quality of the instructors and the fact they really care about your succeeding with the training." Ryan has settled into the program now, but early on he was almost overwhelmed with the pace and amount of learning required in keeping up with the program. "They throw it at you so fast," he said. The popular term among the students for this feeling is "helmet fire."

After the successful completion of Phase II, the student moves into Phase III training. At this point, the training program focuses on training the student for a specific type of aircraft. This could be a fighter, a bomber, a cargo plane, a tanker, a helicopter, or the C-130. The students selected to fly the fighter/bomber track or the tanker/cargo track continue their training at Columbus. Those selected for the C-130 train with the Navy at Corpus Christi, Texas, while the helicopter trainees report for further training with the Army at Fort Rucker, Alabama. Who gets what plane is based upon many factors, some of which are the needs of the Air Force, class rank, and the student's desire.

There are two aircraft used at Columbus Air Force Base during Phase III training, the T-38 and the T-1. The T-38 is used for those who will eventually go into fighters or bombers; the T-1 is used for the future tanker or cargo aircraft pilot.

The Northrop T-38A Talon first entered service in 1961 at Randolph Air Force Base. In this aircraft, student and instructor pilot sit in tandem on ejection seats and have a cockpit with complete instrumentation. The plane has a maximum take-off weight of 12,093 lbs. With a wingspan of about 25 feet, the T-38 has a maximum speed of 858 mph and a service ceiling of 53,600 feet. A total of 1,187 T-38s have been produced for the Air Force, 80 of which are assigned to Columbus Air Force base. This trainer will continue in service for many more years following upgrades to include state of the art instrumentation. The T-38 is more challenging to fly than the T-37, especially in the landing pattern, but it is an excellent lead-in to world class fighter aircraft like the F-16.

The student receives about 115 hours of flying time in the T-38 during the Phase III program. The program is structured like Phase II, where the student builds on what he/she has already learned in Phase II with the T-37 and applies it to the T-38. The categories of instruction are the same; they are contact, instrument, formation, and navigation flying. One part of the training that receives considerable attention and time is formation flying. One of the reasons formation flying is given so much emphasis is that fighter pilots always use this as their normal flight formation primary for mutual protection. Another reason is that for handling purposes a formation of aircraft can be considered as one aircraft. For example when the formation is approaching the base for landing, the controller handles the flight as one ship for purposes of setting up the landing sequence. Formation flying must become second nature to the fighter pilot because he must be able to focus his attention on other flight responsibilities, especially in combat.

During Phase III the student will advance from the two-ship formation to a four-ship formation. This is especially difficult flying and requires considerable skill learned only through practice.

One of the students in the final part of Phase III training was 2nd Lt. Shannon Hodge. Lt. Hodge is from Columbus, Ohio where she graduated from the ROTC program at Ohio State University. She remembers "The hardest part of the program is realizing that you are in a learning environment, and when you get criticized by your instructors that you not take it personally. There's always the pressure of wanting to do well in your training. I like meeting people and the family atmosphere; you want your buddies to do well." Following graduation Hodge will stay at Columbus as an instructor pilot in the T-38. That's a three year assignment after which she hopes to get an opportunity to fly the F-15E Strike Eagle. Looking beyond the F-15, Hodge wants to attend test pilot school and become a test pilot.

The other aircraft used in the Phase III program is the T-1A Jayhawk. Students who are assigned a tanker or cargo plane will train on this aircraft and will fly it about 160 hours during Phase III. Half of that flying time is devoted to flying the plane, while the other half is spent in the jumpseat observing another student pilot while he/she flys. An instructor is always present. The Jayhawk made by the Raytheon Corporation, is a military version of the Beech 400A. Forty-nine are assigned to Columbus Air Force Base. The T-1A has a crew of three, a pilot, co-pilot, and instructor pilot.

Lt. Joseph Coslett, Deputy Chief of Public Affairs for the 14th Flying Training Wing. Lt. Coslett went to considerable time and trouble to set up the author's itinerary and accompanied him during the visit.

2nd Lt. John Poole who was taking Phase III training in the T-1A at the time of the author's visit recalled, "I love the flying part of my instruction, and the opportunity to command. The guys in my class are pretty tight. The hardest part for me has been to prioritize my time, always thinking about how can I best spend my time. Right now I'm looking at spending 20 years in the Air Force, but later on perhaps I'll decide to go into the airlines. This is an awesome opportunity just to be involved." Lt. Poole is a graduate of the Corps of Cadets from Texas A&M, and is the third generation of his family to serve our country in the Air Force. John's grandfather served during WW II, and his father, a doctor, is currently stationed at Columbus Air Force Base; one of his duties is a Flight Surgeon.

During WW II the pilot trainee advanced from Basic flight training to the next phase, which was called Advanced Flight Training. This was similar to today's Phase III program.

In Advanced, the cadet took a 10-week course (1944) which included 70 hours of flying training which was broken into five phases. The phases were transition, instrument, navigation, formation, and aerobatics. Just as in today's Phase III training, WW II advanced training was broken out into single engine or multi-engine training. Single engine trainees typically went on to fighters, and twin engine trainers would fly bombers, transports, or twin engine fighters. Combat experience gave emphasis to formation flying training especially at high altitude using the three-ship V formation. Following the completion of Advanced, the cadet was awarded the wings of an Air Force pilot and commissioned as a 2nd lieutenant or a Flight Officer. Following Advanced training, pilots were assigned additional training in the type of aircraft they would fly in combat. The single engine trainees who were assigned fighters would take an additional five-week course on gunnery and fighter transition.

Just as in World War II, today's students (especially the fighter pilots) must learn to fly the aircraft as if they were an extension of themselves. There is simply no time or opportunity (as in a combat situation) to think of control inputs or basic flight maneuvers. This must be done by instinct so that the attention of the pilot can be given to the accomplishment of his/her mission. It probably takes about a year to learn to fly a specific fighter aircraft well. It takes about two years to learn how to use its complex armament systems with a good degree of competence. Then the procedures must be practiced over and over again in situations as near to the real thing as possible. That's why military flying training is a dangerous, unforgiving business.

In 2001, 443 students entered Phase I training at Columbus Air force Base. Of that number, 320 graduated from Columbus and earned their Silver Wings. Fifty-Four students went onto Corpus Christi, Texas for the C-130 program, and 12 were sent to learn to fly helicopters at Fort Rucker, Alabama. About 13% of the total class did not complete the course. Historically, most of the students drop from the program of their own volition, just one or two percent are "washed out." The majority of students who drop from the program do so during Phase II.

The proud tradition of training the world's best pilots continues today at Columbus Air Force Base. Here, about one third of all the new Air Force pilots receive their initial flight training. An impressive monument located in front of the Wing Headquarters building pays tribute to the graduates of Columbus Air Force Base. It reads: "This monument is dedicated to Columbus Air Force Base pilot training graduates and students who placed nation above self and made the ultimate sacrifice in the service of their country." There are seventy-two names listed on the monument.

The author is deeply indebted to and appreciative of the help given him by the Department of the Air Force and the personnel of Columbus Air Force Base. I especially want to thank, Lieutenant Joseph Coslett, Ms. Connie Lisowski, and Captain Timothy Sundvall for their efforts to help me better understand the flight training of today's Air Force pilot.

Aerial view of Tonopah Army Air Field circa 1944.
(CENTRAL NEVADA HISTORICAL SOCIETY)

Tonopah Army Air Field as it is today. (DAVE)

In the Middle of Nowhere

TONOPAH ARMY AIR FIELD

Upon his arrival at Tonopah Army Air Field in February 1944, Lt. Joe Beckman penned a letter to his parents in Hamilton, Ohio. He wrote, "I never knew there was so much rough barren ground, but this state of Nevada is full of it. Hills and desert with not even trees growing, nothing but brush." Later he would write, "Everything worthwhile is so far away that it takes three days to get anyplace and back. The only two places within three days traveling time are Reno and Las Vegas…"

Another soldier, John Holmgren, spent a year at Tonopah Army Air Field and would later write, "The trip took forever, or so it seemed. I managed to doze off a little and when the train jerked to a stop in Tonopah, I looked out the window and thought I had come through some kind of time warp and was back in the early nineteenth century. The town looked like the setting for a cowboy flick of the Gold Rush Era. I spent almost one year in Tonopah and I never quite got over the feeling of being transported to another era in American history…"

The letters are not exaggerations; Tonopah Army Air Field was indeed isolated. This training base sat in the middle of the high desert of Central Nevada, and was closer to Death Valley than any major population center. The nearest town, Tonopah was just six miles to the west. The town was founded in 1900 as a result of a silver mining boom. By 1940, the mines had all but played out and the town's population had declined from a high of about 11,500 to 2,500, and was struggling to avoid becoming another Nevada ghost town. The building of the air base would prove to be a tremendous economic stimulus not only for Tonopah but also for the entire area.

At first, the base was planned to be a support airport for the gunnery and bombing range that was to be built near Tonopah. The range was huge, 3,500,000 acres, and the airport to support it would also be built near the town. Later, in October 1940, plans became more specific as reported in the local paper, the *Tonopah Daily Times*, in October 1940: "Under present plans outlined to local committee members, the army is scheduled to use the Tonopah range for aerial bombing practice by west coast air squadrons. Construction work includes the establishment of an airport, barracks and other necessary buildings for the operation of the planes during the practice maneuvers. Army officials have indicated that a permanent detachment of 200 enlisted men and four officers will be stationed here with quarters of sufficient size to house a maximum of 1,000 men."

Above: The main entrance to the base as it was around 1944. Note the lighting fixtures on the pillars. They appear to have been made of 100-lb. practice bomb casings and runway lights.
(CENTRAL NEVADA HISTORICAL SOCIETY)

Right: Today's entrance to the field. The lighting fixtures have been replaced and the guard shack is gone.

The airport, later to become a major training base, was built in two phases. The first phase was built under the supervision of the Works Projects Administration (WPA) as part of the national defense program. After much discussion among various officials, government agencies, and politicians, permission to start construction was received via telegram from Washington on November 30th 1940. The first construction was to include a runway, water storage tanks, and clearing and grading of the land. About $185,770 was allocated for this (about $1.9 million in 2002 dollars).

By August 1941, one runway was about finished (it was 7,200 feet long), and plans were being finalized to spend an additional $600,000 to $800,000 for two additional runways. Mean-

while, problems had occurred relative to settling mining issues and the value of property for land in the proposed bombing range. At this point, talks were centered on gaining immediate access to 983,040 acres of land that were located in the center of the range.

It was not until July 2, 1942 that the first group of military personnel arrived at what was to become Tonopah Army Air Field. Included in the group was Lt. Col. Frank Gore (the first commander) and Staff Sgt. Vernon Nightengale. They were part of the 413th Base Headquarters Squadron. Sgt. Nightengale recalled his first impressions of his new office: "The original equipment with which the base was started consisted of 48 sacks of mail, one typewriter, a mess hall stool, and a wooden box. Our first job was to get a scoop and two brooms and sweep out a truck full of dust." Years later, writing for the Central Nevada Museum, he remembers: "Being stationed in San Francisco and coming to a desert valley in Nevada was a change that would test the best of us while stationed at Tonopah. . . . In our first view of the valley, we could see a few scattered temporary buildings and one hangar. About two hundred yards through the main gate, on the left, was a building where base headquarters would locate." To get the headquarters into operation, the men went into town to the local newspaper office and picked up a typewriter, typing paper and a stencil. At this time, there were just two planes on the field, one of which was a BT-14—a two place single engine trainer.

When the base officially opened on July 1, 1942, there were at least 74 buildings in place, which included 50 barracks, 12 BOQs, 11 mess halls, and the hospital with a capacity of 20 beds. At this time it was called the Tonopah Bombing and Gunnery Range Detachment.

There were less than 300 men assigned to the base and the living conditions were primitive. In addition to the stifling heat, dust and dirt seemed to cover everything. The dust was everywhere as a result of being blown around by the ever-present wind. To make matters interesting, there were no water sewage disposal facilities. As a result, deep pit latrines were used, and with the attended odors, caused many who

A bomb target observation tower. The tower was used from 1944 to 1945 to observe practice bomb drops. Later it was moved into Tonopah and used as an announcer stand at the Tonopah High School football field until 1991.

were used to more modern conveniences to wish they were someplace else. Also, rattlesnakes were common, and the men were cautioned not to touch a rabbit carcass because of the danger of rabbit and spotted fever.

On July, 14th, there was a brief base open house and a troop review held on the parade grounds to help introduce the base to the public. There was also a flag raising ceremony. Several hundred people from the base and the town were present along with Senator Pat McCarran of Nevada, who spoke during the occasion. Also present was the Tonopah High School Band, which played the "Star Spangled Banner" during the flag raising ceremony.

When the base first opened, its mission was markedly different than it would be several

A sign used to warn people of the bombing and gunnery range. It was recovered by Allen Metscher and is now on display at the Central Nevada Museum.

Above: Partial view of the swimming pool in the town of Tonopah in use by the cadets for water training.
(CENTRAL NEVADA MUSEUM)

Left: This is all that remains of the pool today.

months later. The Tonopah Bombing and Gunnery Range Detachment was designated as a subbase of March Field, California on July 21, 1942. This was for the purpose of administration and supply only. The mission of the gunnery range at the time was "the maintaining of bombing and gunnery ranges to train fighter pilots, gunners, and bombardiers. The mission of the Base Personnel was to perform the 'housekeeping' activities in an efficient manner to facilitate this training." Later in the war, the main emphasis of the base was the training of heavy bombardment crews flying the B-24 Liberator.

The first tactical unit to be trained at Tonopah was the 42nd Bombardment Detach-ment made up of the 390th Bombardment Squadron and the 75th Bombardment Squadron. The unit left on January 28, 1943 for McChord Field in Washington State. Around this time, December 1942, Lt. Col. Gore moved on to become CO of Muroc Air Base (today's Edwards Air Force Base) and was replaced by Lt. Col. Jacob McGrillis.

The early part of the base history is probably best known for its P-39 training and the impact this training had upon many people who lived near the base. The P-39 is a single engine, single seat, low wing fighter that was made by the Bell Aircraft Corporation. This nimble little fighter had a top speed in excess of 350 miles per hour, but was severely restricted in performance at altitudes in excess of 15,000. Many of these aircraft were used as trainers, the first of

The Mizpah Hotel now closed and for sale. During the period of time when the base was in operation, it was often the only place in Tonopah where a person could get a room. As a result, many of the soldier's families spent their first night here.

Officers from the base using the steps of the Mizpah Hotel for a reviewing stand during a parade in Tonopah during 1944. (CENTRAL NEVADA MUSEUM)

Merle Olmsted (on the right) and his friend Ray Morrison in a picture taken at Tonopah Army Air Field. At the time, Merle was a mechanic with the 357th Fighter Group. Merle's T-shirt reads "Tonopah Bombing and Gunnery Range." Today Mr. Olmsted is a world class aviation writer. (OLMSTED)

which arrived at Tonopah in January 1943 with some squadrons of the 354th Fighter Group. Another group that used the P-39 was the 357th Fighter Group; they arrived in March 1943. Another group, the 367th, stationed at Santa Rosa AAF in California, sent its squadrons to Tonopah for bombing and gunnery training.

In *Central Nevada's Glorious Past,* the newspaper of the Central Nevada Museum Vernon Nightengale writes, "It was like a breath of fresh air when the first P-39 fighter squadrons arrived and they were exciting to see in action, but the base C.O. office was kept busy replying to letters from ranchers, mine owners, etc. registering complaints. The complaints included P-39's buzzing ranches, stock pens, and cattle on the range, as well as bullet holes in mine buildings and equipment. Also residents did not appreciate aircraft playing "follow the leader" over and near Tonopah. Two or three would sweep in lower and lower until they flew just above the houses and up over the pass toward the base."

During 1943, P-39 training activity slowed as the field prepared to convert to its new role of training B-24 crews. By the end of November

1943, the base had trained eight bombardment squadrons and 12 fighter squadrons.

The reason for the change in training status is unclear. Some believe the high altitude of the field (over 5000') and the extreme temperatures in the summer, which easily exceeded 100 degrees, played a role in the decision. These extremes had a negative effect on the P-39's performance. The high accident rate for the young men flying the P-39s may also have been a factor.

The high altitude and temperature (high-density altitude) also played havoc with the performance of the B-24 Liberator, the aircraft that replaced the P-39. Dean Gustavson, who at the time was 2nd Lt. and a pilot of a B-24, wrote his impressions of the field's suitability for B-24 training upon his arrival at Tonopah in June 1944: "Tonopah AAFB was located at an elevation of 5,426 feet, and in the summer the temperatures would climb into the 100 degree Fahrenheit range with a density altitude at 9,500 feet. Under these conditions, the successful operation of a B-24 with a full complement of crew, gas and 100 pound practice bombs became marginal. As a consequence, early morning or nighttime training flights were desired but not always possible." Dean also mentioned that the planes used were "war-wearies," D models with many problems and maintenance deficiencies.

Perhaps one reason for the change in type of training was a function of the desperate need for bomber crews and the growing number of fighter pilots in the already existing training pipeline, at the time.

For whatever reason, the base was shut down in September 1943 in preparation for a huge expansion project that would convert it into a B-24 training center. By mid-October 1943, the population of the base had declined to about 1,750 men. Most of the men were sent to Bishop Army Air Field, just over the border in California, in order to make room for the construction workers who would live in the barracks formerly occupied by the soldiers, and eat in the mess halls which were now run by the contractor.

The completion of the first part of the expansion took about five weeks and was finished on November 1. This was for the priority buildings, and allowed the base to begin training of B-24 crews around November 1. Other construction continued for non-essential buildings, and the entire job was done around December 31, 1943. The base had changed dramatically. Now there were 438 buildings, including 114 barracks, 15 mess halls, and an expanded hospital with a capacity for 260 beds.

The most important part of the work was accomplished under unfavorable weather conditions and in the record time of just five weeks. Some of the major parts of the expansion included the building of an enlarged parking apron that was 600 feet wide and almost a mile long, (4,800 feet). Additionally, two runways were enlarged to 150 feet wide and 8,700 feet long,

and at last, the base received a complete sewage disposal system. To obtain adequate water supplies, it was necessary to dig wells and lay steel pipe from Rye Patch, Nevada to the base, a distance of nine miles. It took just eight days to transport the pipe to the construction site, dig the trench, weld the pipe together and back fill the trench.

In addition to the weather problems, the remoteness of the location caused two other problems, lack of adequate transportation and sufficient workers to do the construction. Transportation was a problem because there were no adequate railroads to service the base. As a result, most of the construction material was trucked to the site. Additionally, there were no workers nearby to handle a construction project this large. The nearest large town was Tonopah and with a 1943 population of just 2,500, the town was not able to furnish workers in any quantity. As a result, it was necessary to recruit workers from California, most of who were unskilled.

The contractors who had signed on to construct the 140 buildings employed about 1,000 laborers that worked one shift. To simplify matters, a mill was set up on the site, where the lumber was precut and many sections prefabricated. As a result, the unskilled labor did very little cutting and most of their time was spent nailing pieces together. To help train the unskilled workers, 200 experienced men, spread out among the unskilled workers answering questions and directing their efforts when necessary.

The expansion made the base a much more livable location; there were now bowling alleys, movie theatres, and expanded base recreational facilities. It was still isolated, barren, and lonely. Adequate housing for off base personnel was very limited, and because of this, the service men were encouraged not to bring their wives and children. Still, they did.

As late as February 1945 (two months before the end of the war in Germany) newly arriving military dependents were forced to spend nights in the Nye county courthouse jail because

A dance underway at Tonopah circa 1944.
(CENTRAL NEVADA MUSEUM)

Two of the three remaining hangars at Tonopah AAF as they are today.

of the lack of rooms. In the courthouse, the second story cell block was set aside as temporary housing for the wives and children of airmen stationed at Tonopah Army Air Field. Unfortunately, they had to be locked in at night to protect them from the prisoners who were on the first floor. Some of the dependents lived there for weeks because there was no where else to go. Some found rooms in the Goldfield Hotel located in the small town of Goldfield, about 30 miles south of Tonopah.

Warren Roquet was stationed at Tonopah for navigator training in the winter of 1944–45. He and his new bride, Gwen were lucky. Gwen joined him in Tonopah after spending her first night in town at the jailhouse. Later she moved into the Goldfield hotel before they found an upstairs room with a bath in a private home in Tonopah. Warren remembered that others were not so fortunate: "Few others were so well housed. Enlisted personnel and their families sometimes lived in buildings that had been abandoned for years and were rehabilitated by nailing chicken wire over the inside walls and then covering the wire with cardboard. Various kinds of coal oil heaters made the places barely livable. Most plumbing was outdoors." Another example of the wretched living conditions for some of the men was a "home" lived in by a navigator, his wife and baby. The dwelling was

The author's younger son, Chip and Allen Metscher with one of the three remaining hangars in the background.

a single room in a former chicken house. It had a dirt floor with whitewashed walls, and was lighted by a single bulb that hung from the ceiling. The only water in the room came from a cold water tap.

The income at least for the single officers, was not a hardship. Joe Beckman wrote to his parents from Tonopah in April 1944: "As to my monthly paychecks, they amount to $150.00

base pay, plus $75.00 flying pay, plus $21.00 for food minus about $6.00 for insurance. Giving me a total of $240.00 income a month. My meals which amount to a dollar a day or so, and $6.00 Officer Club and B.O.Q. dues are the only expenses I have other than laundry and pleasure." Joe Beckman would finish his navigator training and go to the Far East where he would fly 55 combat missions in B-24s bombing Japanese targets. Following the war, he entered the seminary and today serves as a Roman Catholic priest in Cincinnati, Ohio.

Training resumed on November 1, when the soldiers returned from Bishop Army Air Field. About the same time, the 458th Bombardment Group arrived for second and third phase training. The group, which consisted of 260 Officers and 1,064 Enlisted men, arrived by train at Mina, Nevada (population 400) and were transported by truck to the base.

The morale of the men stationed at Tonopah Army Air Field was never very high, especially during the months of 1943 and early 1944. Two key reasons were the isolation of the post coupled with the poor housing conditions off base. The low morale was reflected in the performance of the men, especially in the area of maintenance. Making the maintenance situation worse were the worn out B-24s that were used early in the training program. As a result, crashes due to equipment malfunction were all too frequent.

Apparently the situation did not improve, because in April 1944 the base received an unsatisfactory rating by inspectors from the 4th Air Force and other inspection teams. Additional inspections followed, probably the most important was a short two hour visit made on Saturday May 20th by General William Lynd, Commanding General of the Fourth Air Force. He

Top: The remains of an operations board inside one the hangars. Above: A view looking up to the roof of a hangar. Note the all-wood construction.

looked at flight training and aircraft maintenance. Other inspections made during May 22 thru May 24 centered on personnel and their duties performed. Apparently the inspections did not go well, because on May 26, Col. McCrillis was relieved of command and replaced by Col. Elder Patteson.

Col. Patteson was here for only a short time, May 27, 1944 to June 7, 1944, after which he left to attend the Army War College. One of the first things he did was to start a post-landscaping plan. Over a period of months, improvements

The base hospital circa 1943. This was before the base beautification program began. Note the covered walkways between the buildings. (CENTRAL NEVADA HISTORICAL SOCIETY)

were made to the post, such as the planting of grass, trees, and shrubs.

Col. Stanton T. Smith arrived on the base on June 16 to replace him. Vernon Nightengale, who was Sergeant Major of the base headquarters at the time, remembers the situation well. Writing in the publication *Central Nevada's Glorious Past* he recalled… "The word was that Col. Smith was a hard nose with the 'all Army or nothing' attitude. He put all section staff on notice to be prepared to ship out if immediate improvements were not accomplished." During the time Col. Smith commanded

The interior of the post exchange restaurant. With no central heat and air conditioning, it was probably very hot in the summer and chilly in the winter.
(CENTRAL NEVADA HISTORICAL SOCIETY

Tonopah Army Air Field, he did not live on the base. Instead, he lived in the small town of Bishop, California about 112 miles west of Tonopah. It was unusual for a base commander to live off base, and the fact that he did so did not lend itself to improving morale.

The personnel of the Fourth Air Force made additional inspections and in July the training center received a "satisfactory" rating; the situation was starting to improve. The base history report for July 1944 said, "The improvement in all lines is very noticeable by the personnel stationed here.... messes have improved, ratings have started to blossom forth, organizations and individuals are being recognized for their activities and with this, morale has increased to a great extent.... Those who have been stationed here for some time have completely lost that feeling of being cast out and now realize the importance of the mission ..." At this time (August 1944), there were an average of 66 B-24s assigned to the base, of which 21 were flyable. The training of B-24 crews had reached its peak, and this was reflected in the average number of officers and enlisted men assigned to the base; the officers numbered 1,083 and the enlisted men 5,350.

One of the more innovative morale building activities begun during Col. Smith's command was the building of a recreation center at June Lake, California in

Many foundations remain at the former training field. This is a foundation for a movie theatre.

July 1944. The camp, located about sixty miles from Bishop, California, had facilities for fishing, boating, horse-back riding, swimming, and hiking in the summer, and hunting, skiing, ice-skating, etc. in the winter. The *Desert Bomber*, the post newspaper, described it as being, "Among the snow-capped mountains in the high Sierras ... a total change of scenery, impressive mountains, a lake fed by mountain freshets and plenty of trees to give you privacy." The only drawback was its limited accommodations—33 enlisted men and 10 officers. The normal period of stay was four days.

Col. Smith remained in command of Tonopah Army Air Field until December 5, 1944 at which time Col. John Feagin replaced him. Col. Smith was reassigned to March Field, California as commanding officer of that field. The new commander, Col. Feagin continued the morale building efforts started by the former commanders, Cols. Patteson and Smith. One of his more innovative efforts was the starting of a column in the weekly edition of the post newspaper, the *Desert Bomber*. The column titled "If I were CO" aired suggestions and gripes from the base personnel, which in turn were answered by the Colonel. Many of the complaints centered on the poor off base housing situation (which was never corrected) and problems with the Post Exchange system (quality of food, hours open for business and the variety of merchandise). Another writer suggested the Col. attend chapel services. Not all comments were gripes; one sergeant wrote in July 1945... "No gripes this time: Just thanks for making this place fit to live in."

Over time, the efforts to improve the morale and performance of the men and women of the base resulted in much improved results. For example, in April 1945 the base set a new safety record for the Fourth Air Force by flying 33,500 hours without a fatal accident. Towards the end of May, Tonopah Army Air Base set another record in the Fourth Air Force by flying 51,505 hours without a fatal accident. Clearly the men and women of the training center were huge factors in this excellent performance; however, there were other factors also at work. The most important was the training aircraft. By this time, late in the war, they were in much better condition, some fresh from the factory. Parts were more available, and the conditions under which the mechanics labored were much improved. Finally, the frantic rush to prepare men for combat was over, and there was more time allocated for training.

In addition to the training of B-24 bomber

The author's older son Dave on the ramp at Tonopah.

crews, there was considerable secret research and testing done at Tonopah on guided bomb systems. The Material Command, Special Weapons Branch at Wright Field, in Dayton Ohio took a special interest in the Tonopah area. During early 1944, test teams began arriving at Tonopah Army Air Field and were assigned a hangar on the south end of the base.

The primary purpose of the unit was the research, testing and experimentation of glide bombs. These were the forerunners of today's smart bombs. Over the next several months there were three different types of guidance systems tested on different versions of glide bombs. The glide bombs were designated as the GB-4, the GB-6 and the GB-8.

The GB-4 had a primitive TV camera hanging under a 2,000-lb. bomb that was attached to a glide mechanism. This TV camera enabled the person guiding the bomb to fly it into the target by watching a small TV screen in the mother ship. The GB-6 utilized a heat seeking system to find its target, and the GB-8 was a radio-controlled bomb. Also tested near Tonopah was the VB-6, a high angle heat-seeking bomb.

The number of personnel assigned to Tonopah for this work was not large, about 25 officers and 65 enlisted men. The aircraft used during the tests were the B-17, B-25, AT-7, and

This is what's left of the ditching pool at Tonopah. Constructed later in the war, and filled with water, it contained a fuselage of an aircraft. This was used as a training device to teach airmen how to evacuate an aircraft after a water landing.

The remains of bunkers used to store ammunition and bombs used in training.

a PQ-8. The PQ-8 was a single engine, one-man aircraft built by Culver Aircraft Company. The AT-7 had a Thermopile Infrared Detector mounted in its nose. This device was used to detect the heat output of targets during the tests. The special unit continued its work at Tonopah until October 1944, after which it relocated to Wendover Field in Utah.

Prior to the unit relocating to Wendover, two C-54s (military version of the DC-4) were loaded with GB4 and GB8 parts and flown to England. After much confusion relative to the nature and knowledge of the project, several GB4s and GB8 were assembled and made ready to drop on specially selected targets. In August 1944, three GB4s (television guided bombs) were dropped on submarine pens in France. All missed. Later in September, a more successful use of a GB4 was achieved when the bomb was steered into a tree. It was diverted from its original target because the operator believed the building was a schoolhouse, so he put the bomb into a tree next to the building. This was a chilling forerunner of the accuracy that would be achieved almost 50 years later.

As a side note to this episode of Tonopah history, it's interesting to note that historian, and aviation archaeologist, Allen Metscher, has found and restored several components of these early bombs. Mr. Metscher combed the former testing sites of these bombs near Tonopah, and found many of their parts. After discussions with the personnel involved in the testing program, he reassembled them, and today they are on display in the Central Nevada Museum.

After V-J Day, rumors began circulating that the base would soon close. The rumors were true, because on August 23, 1945, the base was placed on temporary inactive status. On August 26 all training classes were stopped, and flying training for combat crews was stopped soon after. By September 15, just four aircraft remained of the 75 assigned to the field. A month later, on October 15, the base was designated a sub-base of Hamilton Field, California. Additional changes occurred over the following months, and by August 1946, there were just 66 officers and men on the field. Tonopah Army Air Field, which once was bursting with activity, training thousands of crewmembers, was now just another Nevada ghost town.

Today, the field serves the city of Tonopah and Nye County, Nevada. Occasionally the Air Force is involved in activity here because of the field's close proximately to various test and bombing ranges. Two runways are still in use, the longer of which is 7,100 feet long. A visitor will find that some of the field remains from its World War II service. Three hangars are still here, as are the foundations of many buildings and a few streets.

The person most familiar with the proud history of this training center is Allen Metscher. He, along with his two brothers, Bill and Phil, founded the Central Nevada Historical Society, which has gained national recognition as an authority on Western history. Allen's specialty is the history of the former base, and to that end he has done exhaustive research on the subject, including contacting the people who served there and recording their experiences for future historians. Additionally, he has combed the desert for artifacts and located the crash sites of many aircraft that went down while training at the field. More importantly, he has built monuments to the men and women who served at Tonopah and erected memorial markers near the crash sites of many planes. One of the memorials erected by Mr. Metscher contains the names of the 117 men known to have been killed while at Tonopah, most of which were the result of P-39 and B-24 crashes.

Much of this research and artifacts can be seen in the museum in Tonopah also founded by Allen and his two brothers. The Central Nevada Museum, located at 1900 Logan Field Road in Tonopah, is one of the finest in this part of the country. Much of the information in this story of Tonopah Army Air Base is the result of Allen's research and writings.

Allen Metscher standing in front of one of the monuments he built honoring the men and women who served at Tonopah AAF. The particular monument has relics recovered from a crash site and includes a 50cal. machine gun, engine, and prop blade. Engraved on the monument are the names of the known killed in aircraft accidents at Tonopah AAF.

10

"Save our Base"

REESE AIR FORCE BASE

I first met Alan Henry, the former mayor of Lubbock, Texas in his office just on the outskirts of Lubbock. While talking about the closing of Reese Air Force Base, he said "It was fortunate that the economy was good when Reese was phased out. Many said that 'it wasn't a big deal' but it was. Maybe dollar and cents wise we'll be even, but what we lost was the flavor of the military—all those young pilots and their families." His thoughts were common to most of the folks I talked with. The people of Lubbock had a strong affection for the men and women of Reese and pride in the pilots that trained there.

A 1997 edition of the local paper, *The Avalanche-Journal* commented:

> Since February 1995, when word reached the public that Reese Air Force Base was in peril, many Lubbockites have looked forward to today with anxiety, dread and disbelief. The day many prayed would not arrive is here... The announcement two years ago that Reese may be on the Pentagon's hit list sparked months of frenzied planning rallying and organizing by Lubbock City leaders and congressional representatives.

Four members of the Base Closure and Realignment Commission toured the base in April—a visit that city leaders prepared for zealously. They told residents, business owners and media to give the group a greeting they would not forget. Even they did not anticipate the outpouring of support by residents. Yellow ribbons adorned fences, trees and fire engines. Motorists drove with their lights on, and about 80 residents greeted the BRAC commissioners at the airport. Thousands lined the streets along the commissioner's path, shouting and waving yellow ribbons and signs that read "Stand Up for Reese," and "Save Reese." Students were released from classes to greet the group. Reese Elementary students chanted, "Save our Base" for 30 minutes as commissioners passed.

One board member was moved to tears by the city's demonstration. Two months later, the commission voted 6–2 to close the gates of Reese Air Force Base.

Reese AFB is located on the high plains of west central Texas, and since 1942 has been training pilots. The base was officially dedicated on June 21, 1942, but had already turned out its first pilot class of 73 students (Class 42-D) in April 1942. They were single engine pilots. During that war, the base had three names. At first it was called the Air Corps Advanced Flying School, then in late 1941 or early 1942, the name

141

An aerial view of Reese Air Force Base as it appeared around 1945. Note the triangular runway system. (USAF)

Partial view of the inactivation ceremony on September 30, 1997. Officer behind podium is Col. Henry Horton who was commander of the 64th Flying Training Wing at Reese. Col. Horton was one of four pilots who flew Reese's last two planes to Laughlin Air Force Base in Del Rio, Texas. (USAF)

This picture taken in the '70s shows a much larger base with a redesigned runway system. The longer runways were required to accommodate the needs of higher performance aircraft. The area at the top of the picture, across the road, is Reese Village. This was a military housing complex that had 232 buildings containing 400 housing units. Today the buildings are in the process of being sold to civilian owners. (USAF)

was changed to Lubbock Army Flying School, and finally Lubbock Army Air Field. The field would train 7,009 pilots during that war, most learned to fly twin engine aircraft.

In November 1949, the base was renamed Reese Air Force Base to honor the memory of Augustus Reese Jr. who was killed in a bombing mission over Sardinia, Italy in May 13, 1943. Lt. Reese was flying a P-38 during an attack on an enemy supply train. His aircraft was caught up in the explosion of the train and crashed killing the young officer. His sister, Katherine Reese Shep-

herd, who was 20 years old when her brother was killed, was able to attend the closing ceremonies of the base on September 30, 1997.

The last class (97-04) graduated Reese Air Force Base on January 24, 1997. During this last phase of its operation, the field had about 200 aircraft that were used in the Joint Specialized Undergraduate Pilot Training program. Three types of aircraft were used in the program, the T-37, T-38, the T-1. From the first to the last graduating class the school had trained a total of 25,349 pilots.

When the base closed in September 1997, it was situated on about 3,000 acres and had a total of approximately 700 buildings. It was city unto itself that included a housing development of 232 homes, called Reese Village, and a school. As this is being written, the school is empty, the playground deserted, and the homes are slowly being dismantled and trucked away. The quality of life at this airbase was good, and the men and women of the Air Force enjoyed living and working here.

Today, the former air base is called Reese Technology Center and is developing its goal of becoming a master-planned research and business park. Located here are units of Texas Tech University and South Plains College as well as business and community-related enterprises.

Partial view of the mall leading to the base headquarters. The first aircraft is a T-38 and the one behind it is the T-37. Both were used in the training program at Reese. Following base closure, the aircraft were removed. Local citizen effort, which included the former mayor of Lubbock, Alan Henry, saw the plane placed on a pylon in front of a local interactive museum called the Science Spectrum Center. (USAF)

Another aircraft proudly displayed on a pylon was this B-25. This plane had been on display near the base entrance since 1959, and was dedicated to Col. Edgar McElroy, a Lubbock resident who flew the 13th aircraft in the Doolittle Raid. Attempts to retain the plane for display in the Lubbock area were not successful, and it was moved to the Admiral Nimitz Museum, Fredericksburg, Virginia. Here it will go on display to commemorate the Doolittle Raid on Tokyo. (USAF)

Above: The base headquarters building now being used for various offices. The grassy area leading to the building once contained several aircraft on pylons, later removed when the base reverted to civilian control. At the foot of the three flag poles is a small monument that honors the history of Reese Air Force Base. The plaque reads: "On 30 September 1997, Reese Air Force Base and the 64th Flying Training Wing were inactivated culminating a tradition of "55 years of excellence" in serving our nation. Since 1942, 25,349 of the world's greatest pilots graduated from here and the training and support they received from Base personnel and the men and women of the South Plains was unmatched. Reese Air Force Base may be closed, but our legacy will live forever!" Colonel Henry W. "Kodak" Horton, Commander

The control tower. Note the impressions in the paint from the lettering on the tower. It reads, "Reese AFB."

View from the control tower. Most of the equipment has been removed.

This was the largest hangar at Reese AFB, and was often used as the location for ceremonial events.

Another hangar at the former air force base, this one dates back to World War II.

Looking down the flight line several hangars can be seen along with the control tower at the end.

Found at the rear entrance to the former base head-quarters building, this mat announces the headquarters for the 64th Flying Training Wing. Thankfully, many items of this type are being preserved through the efforts of Allen Henry and his associates.

One of the few World War II structures remaining at the former air base. Initially used as a barracks, its last use was as a NCO training school.

Across the road from the base was the military housing complex named Reese Village. Today the homes are being sold to civilian buyers, and the houses moved off the base. This road meanders through the area. Some of the former homes can be seen as they are being prepared for removal.

Above: A view of one of the homes used by the families assigned to the base. This was a two-family home. Left: A children's playground in the former housing area. Today it sits empty and quiet.

A partial view of a kitchen in a model home. These homes were maintained in the condition in which they were vacated in order to show potential buyers.

A liquidation sale sign posted on a building on the flight line. Some of the announcements of items for sale include, "built in range, $400 a set—overhead microwave- like new," GE and Whirlpool new overhead microwaves—$75–100 for sale," "100's Bedframes $15.00," "Small dinette set table/w 2 chairs $60.00 —Many more dinette sets."

Mr. Lyle Hopkins, Operations Supervisor for the Lubbock Reese Redevelopment Authority, inside the former NCO Club. Mr. Hopkins was a career Air Force Noncommissioned Officer and served at Reese Air Force Base. He is pointing out his former rank, that of a Master Sergeant.

Right: The base is closed, and so is the post office

A mural just off the entrance to the maintenance hangar. Pictured are a T-37 and a T-38.

The former main gate to Reese Air Force Base.

Interior view of the hangar loft, and the room where the parachutes are repacked.

The Base Operations building with the sign still intact.

This was
the base
commander's
home.

Bartlett Hall—this
building was used for
NCO quarters.

The Base Commissary.

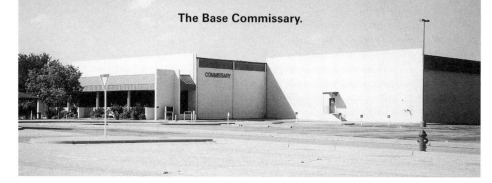

The hospital.

The Post Theatre.

The former chapel, now being used as an activity center for South Plains College.

Sitting in boxes near the former T-1 hangar are pieces of surplus equipment awaiting proper disposal.

This sign seems to say it all. (USAF)

11

Leftover Field

Wendover Army Air Base

The largest military expansion program in United States history had been completed by the end of 1943, and the results could be seen nationwide. There were now 345 major Air Force installations along with 116 sub-bases, and 322 auxiliary landing fields. Most of these bases were used for training and were intended for short-term use.

Typically, the base buildings were simple one or two story wood frame structures with several things in common; they were quick and easy to build and were not intended to be permanent. A common saying is that the buildings were designed to last one day longer than the war. Actually, considering the rush to build the structures and the material with which they were built, the buildings served their purpose well. Even though it's been 60 years since the last of these buildings went up, hundreds still exist across the United States.

Sadly, no complete example of a temporary training base still exists. There are, however, bits and pieces still remaining. Like looking for the remains of a forgotten ghost town, a determined search at the location of a former training base often turns up fascinating remnants of the base. This is often true at locations where the training facility was built far away from major population centers.

Typically, a visitor to a former training base will find the runways intact but grown over with weeds and brush, or the runways are being used as a foundation for modern industrial buildings. Often, the runways are maintained and still in use. In those cases, the hangars may still remain, and they are generally in surprisingly good condition. Many of the building foundations remain, and are typically concrete slabs that resist easy removal. Sometimes, the remains of the storage vaults used to safeguard the then secret Norden bombsights still exist. The buildings that housed the vaults are gone, but the steel reinforced heavy concrete vaults are still in place because they are so difficult to remove. Generally, they sit in lonely isolation in the middle of a field that had once been filled with other buildings. A knowledgeable person can often determine the type of building that once existed simply by looking at the foundation remains.

One of the most intact complete examples of an Army Air Forces training field is Wendover Field in Utah. It is also one of the most historic. Located in northwest Utah, the field is still isolated, sitting in the middle of a vast wasteland miles away from any major population center. It is probably for this reason, and the dry hot climate, that so much remains today. Addition-

Left: Wendover Army Air Base circa 1943. At the bottom of the photo is the area that would later become the technical site. The structures to the extreme right are ammo bunkers. At the base of the mountains is the cantonment area. Note the nose of the B-17 in the upper right corner of the picture. (PETERSEN)

Below: Compare this view (1996) of the former air base with the one taken in 1944. Very little has changed.

ally, the field was used off and on by the Air Force following the war, and over the years, several groups have attempted to preserve the site. About 80 buildings still remain.

The vast runway system still exists as do the hangars and operation's buildings. Most of the hospital complex and many barracks remain, as does a mess hall, chapel, swimming pool, and other buildings. The structure and vaults used to store the Norden bombsights is complete and the vaults retain their original manufacturer markings. The control tower is still in use and overlooks the remains of the formerly highly secret and restricted "technical site" where components of the first atom bombs were assembled. One of the two hangars that housed the B-29s of the famed 509th Composite Bomb Group is still here along with a few of the especially constructed pits where the prototype atom bombs were loaded into the aircraft. There is a lot more to see, especially now that a local group, Historic Wendover Airfield, is hard at work preserving the former base.

During World War II, Wendover Field had several unofficial names. One of the more descriptive was "Leftover Field," a name given it by Bob Hope when he was on an USO tour visiting the air field. Bing Crosby also visited here and called the nearby town, "Tobacco Road with slot machines." The town is named Wendover, and at the time of the airfield's construction it had one paved road (State Route US 40) and a population of about 100 people. The town was right on the border of Utah and Nevada. Nevada allowed gambling. Utah did not. The larg-

Another view showing the hangar row and ramp. The three major groups of buildings behind the flight line and in the upper right of the photo are the remains of the former hospital complex and the barracks. The dry air along with the work of interested people has helped keep the buildings in a remarkable state of preservation.

Two views of today's hangar row with most of the hangars from WW II still intact. Here the B-17s, B-24s, P-47s and finally the B-29s of the 509th Composite Group were housed. The dome-shaped structure was one of two hangars built to house the B-29s. (PETERSEN)

Salt Lake region, was secluded and lonely. Though isolated, the town was served by the Western Pacific Railroad, and many of its citizens were employees of the railroad. Other important factors in locating the base included the Army's intention to convert Fort Douglas (an infantry post at Salt Lake City) into an Air Corps facility, and to use Salt Lake's airport as a field for heavy bombers. But this didn't happen because of the danger of keeping large quantities of high explosives near the city. Prior to this, the explosives were stored at Salt Lake's airport and practice bombing runs were made over the Salt Lake Desert by planes stationed at the airport. So, it made sense to eventually move the planes and armaments out to the more remote site.

There were several stages in the building of the airfield at Wendover. The first part started in November, 1940 with a gravel runway system and just a few buildings. By the end of 1941, the field had been expanded with additional buildings and paved runways. This was the con-

est most active commercial enterprise was the State Line Hotel, which as the name implies, was located right on the state line. There, a customer could walk in the Utah side, have a meal then go through a door into the Nevada side and gamble. The base was located in Utah and was easy walking distance from the town.

A few years after construction first started, during the early 1940s, this isolated, unknown field became the world's largest military base. It also became a training site that would help train and launch the crews that would drop the world's first atom bomb. Today, part of this field, located about one-quarter mile south of the city of Wendover, Utah is listed on the National Register of Historic Places.

The field's history begins in 1940 when the Air Corps was looking for bombing and gunnery ranges. The area near the town of Wendover was well suited to fit these needs. The land was virtually uninhabited, had generally excellent flying weather, and the nearest large city (Salt Lake City) was 100 miles away. The land, part of the huge, wide-open expanse of the Great

The Commemorative Air Force B-29 'FiFi' sitting on the ramp in front of the WW II hangar built for the B-29s. This was on the occasion of the reunion for the 509th Composite Group held in August 2001. Today this hangar is referred to as the Enola Gay Hangar (PETERSEN)

A partial view of some base buildings circa 1943. (PETERSEN)

dition of the field when the first military personnel, about twelve men, arrived in August, 1941. In this group of men was a gunnery and bombing detachment. Facilities were Spartan, with just a few barracks, officer's quarters, and a mess hall. There were also some warehouses, a theater, a medical facility, and a few other buildings located on the field. At this time, the location was used as a bombing range. The installation became a sub-base of Fort Douglas on July 29, 1941, and in March, 1942 was officially recognized as a separate air base. A major expansion program began in 1942 and a total of 668 buildings were constructed. Almost all were wood frame buildings designed to be built with the least expenditure of time and material. Included in the expansion program was a 300-bed hospital, a gymnasium, library, chapel, bowling alley, swimming pool and housing units for married officers and civilians. The largest part of this building project was completed at the end of 1943. At the time, there were a total of about 19,500 military personnel and civilians on the base. By now, Wendover Field had 3,500,000 acres and was the world's largest military reservation.

The training of B-17 and B-24 bomb groups began in April 1942, with the arrival of the 306th Bomb Group flying B-17s. They were in for a rude surprise; there were few training facilities, and the living conditions were primitive. The base had less than 12 buildings to house the bomb group. Conditions were so basic that the same room was used as a headquarters for the bomb group and the individual squadrons. Fifty to sixty men worked just inches apart at a series of small tables that were arranged in a "U" shape. The tables were just boards put over carpenter's horses, and old cardboard boxes were used as filing cabinets. Sometimes, the men had to do their own construction work. For example, they built their own USO center with the help of people living in the towns around the base. The center was constructed in one day and was in use the same night. Range facilities were austere but were expanded over time. This included the building of life-sized targets of battleships, the installation of night lighting, and the construction of rifle, skeet, and machine gun ranges into the hills about four miles from the base. Not all these facilities were available for the 306th Bombardment Group, the first group to train here.

Some of the barracks buildings that remain from World War II. These were called "Theatre of Operations" type buildings and were of temporary construction. Each building housed 24 men. (PETERSEN)

An interior view of an enlisted men's barracks. Note the potbellied stove and the absence of any kind of installation. The buildings were hot and dusty in the summer and cold in the winter.
(PETERSEN)

Another view of some base buildings remaining today. (PETERSEN)

158

Just a short distance from the base and across the state line in Nevada was located the State Line Service Hotel. In addition to lodging and meals, the hotel offered gambling. (PETERSEN)

Wendover's mission was to train heavy bomb groups. At the time, heavy bomb groups were using either the B-17 or the B-24. As with the other training programs throughout the Air Forces, the training of the bomb groups was constantly being changed and modified. Originally there was little experience, few qualified personnel, and precious little equipment. Over time this changed, and as it did, so did the training programs. In March 1942, heavy bomber training was a two-phase program, with each phase being six weeks long. Later, the training was changed to a three-phase program, and each stage lasted four weeks. Wendover would do the second phase training. As mentioned, the first bombardment group to train at Wendover was the 306th, which arrived at the field in April 1942 for training with the B-17. Later on, B-24 groups would train at Wendover. In total, 21 bomb groups and over 1,000 aircrews trained at Wendover.

During 1944, the system that required different bases for different parts of training was changed. Now, all phases of training would be given at the same Operational Training

Unit (OTU) station. Wendover continued its group training under the new system. This training stressed the importance of teamwork and included high altitude formation flying, long-range navigation, target identification, and simulated combat missions.

For a short time, beginning in May 1944, the field trained fighter groups; however, this was abruptly canceled in September 1944. During that period the 72nd Fighter Wing was at Wendover with their P-47s. In September, B-29s arrived on the field, as part of an operation code named "Silver Plate." They would begin preparations for the dropping of the world's first atom bomb in August 1945. This operation and everything connected with it required utmost secrecy. The base itself was given the code name "Kingman," and the activity to assemble, modify

In October 1944 a detachment of the Special Weapons Branch, Wright Field, Ohio arrived at Wendover to evaluate captured experimental rocket systems. This was either a captured German V-1 "buzz bomb" or a copy. (PETERSEN)

159

Above: This shows how the loading pits were used to load the oversize bombs into the bomb bay of the B-29s. (PETERSEN)

Left: An interior view of the bombsight storage building as it appears today. Note the five separate safes with their massive steel doors.

and flight test prototype bombs was code named "Project W-47." The only flying unit on the field was the 393rd Bombardment Squadron, which would later become part of the 509th Composite Group.

As part of the buildup of the 509th Composite Group, about 800 people stationed at the field, were transferred into the group and began training. Some of the other units transferred were the 390th Air Service Group, the 320th Troop Carrier Squadron (the "Green Hornet Airlines"), the 1395th Military Police Company, and later the 1st Ordnance Squadron. In addition, qualified personnel throughout the military were filtered into the group. Only the commander of the group, Colonel Paul W. Tibbets, had full knowledge of its mission. Security was so intense,

that 400 FBI agents were involved to help maintain it. Personnel were instructed to talk with no one about their activities, not even among themselves. Those who did were immediately transferred from Wendover to other assignments, some as far away as Alaska. Most of the 509th Composite Group's training (which included individual as well as crew training) was done at Wendover. Crews were trained to drop one bomb with a high degree of precision, and to execute a sharp turn after dropping it in order to avoid the effects of the nuclear blast. These practice bombs were called "pumpkins" because some were painted orange, and because one of the two types being tested had a round shape. After completing the training at Wendover, the 509th went to Tinian Island. From here, the group continued to drop the pumpkins (which now contained high explosives) over Japan while awaiting the atom bomb.

Left: A view of one of the prototype atom bombs loaded on a trailer ready for transportation to a B-29 for a drop test. The round shape and orange color of this particular bomb caused it to be called a "Pumpkin." Below: A bomb being loaded into the bomb loading pit. The pits were necessary because the bombs were too large to be loaded directly into the aircraft from underneath the plane.
(PETERSEN)

The story of Project W-47 is not well known and is somewhat controversial. The story begins in the ordnance area, which was located on the south side of Wendover Field far away from the main body of the other base buildings. The two areas were separated by the base runway system and joined by dirt and/or cinder roads. The ordnance area consisted of several wooden and metal frame buildings, with no running water and no inside plumbing. Also located within the area were some igloos for the storage of explosives. Later on, additional buildings were constructed which became explosive assembly buildings. Outside the ordnance area were the two sets of pits used to load the oversize bombs into the specially modified B-29s. One set of pits was located on the northwest part of the aircraft parking ramp and the other set was found on the taxi strip on the west side of the field. The area was so isolated that the men working at the site were transported back to the main base for meals. This was the situation in May 1945 when Captain James L. Rowe became project officer in the area now being called the technical area.

At the time, little was known about the flight characteristics of the prototype atom bomb designs and how the fusing mechanism would work. The prototype bombs were assembled at the technical site by men, most of whom had little or no technical experience. So secret was this work that Captain Rowe had virtually no contact with his military superiors, except a monthly visit from a representative of the Joint Chiefs of Staff. Captain Rowe's group worked 24 hours a day, six days a week helping perfect the design of the prototype bombs, later called Fat Man and Little Boy. Much of the technical work was done outside the site but the prototype bombs were assembled there. Once assembled they were loaded into specially modified B-29s and then dropped over Wendover's bombing ranges and elsewhere. The flight characteristics of the bomb would be noted, analyzed at a different location by scientists, and changes in design would be ordered. It is at this point that the story of Project W-47 becomes a bit controversial. According to Captain Rowe, the final assembly of the two atom bombs dropped over Japan took place at Wendover Field. A full and fascinating story of this part of Wendover's history can be found in *Project W-47*, by James L. Rowe, published in 1978 by Ja A Ro Publishing, Livermore, California.

161

Top: A view of a bomb-loading pit as it appears today. There were five of these pits at Wendover, all of which were used to load the prototype atom bombs into the B-29s. Bottom: Another view of a bomb-loading pit as it is being cleaned out of more than 50 years of dirt and debris by Boy Scout Troop 725. During the cleanup of the pit, 40 rounds of live 50-cal. ammunition were found. (PETERSEN)

The training of B-29 aircrews and the testing of prototype atom bombs was the last major contribution of Wendover Field during WW II. After the end of the war with Japan, some crew training continued, but at a reduced level. For a while, B-29s were stored here. Among other things, some work was done with the Air Material Command's weapons development program that included the testing and development of missiles. Some of these missiles were German V-2 rockets that had been confiscated and then sent to Wendover. For a short time, the Strategic Air Command used the field and its ranges for training. In 1948, the base was deactivated and then declared surplus in 1949. Later in 1955, while the field was being used by SAC and the Ninth Air Force, work was done to update some of the facilities. The base was again deactivated in 1957, and the next month renamed Wendover Air Force Auxiliary Field. It was used from time to time by various Air Force units for gunnery practice and summer encampments, among other things. In 1960, the field was placed in caretaker status under the management of Hill Air Force Base, located near Salt Lake City, Utah. Wendover Field was again reactivated in 1961 with only a fire protection group of 15 men stationed on the base. Some of the buildings were removed, and by 1962 only 128 of the original 668 buildings remained. The base was again declared surplus. The government was willing to sell the base and retain the bombing ranges and radar site. At this time, the City of Wendover, now with a population of 800, sought to interest commercial firms in the base. This was not successful, however, and a small crew of civilian fire fighters remained until 1977. Meanwhile, various Air Force units used the facilities from time to time on a temporary basis. The field was again declared surplus in 1972. Earlier, the ranges had been incorporated into the Hill Air Force Base range complex. In July 1975, the base was officially listed on the National Register of Historic Places. In 1977, the government deeded much of the old field to the City of Wendover. This included the runways, the former hospital complex and hangars. Some acres including the radar site were retained by the military. In the late 1990s the base ownership was transferred from Wendover, Utah to Tooele County, Utah.

Today, the field is an active airport serving the nearby town of Wendover. In addition to the

A B-24 that didn't fare well in a forced landing. The nose has been crushed and all four props torn from their engines. (PETERSEN)

buildings mentioned earlier, others remain from WW II, including the first headquarters and a Link trainer building. Scattered about are several attractive informational signs placed at various locations around the former base. These signs help the visitor better understand the role the field played toward speeding the end of WWII. Inside the small but growing museum is an excellent diorama of the field as it appeared during the time when the 509th Bombardment Group was here.

Recently, a new preservation group has been formed by Mr. James Petersen, who is hard at work preserving the field's history. Mr. Petersen first became aware of the base while practicing for his private pilot's license. One of the practice training areas was Wendover Airport. He recalls: "the wide open spaces, clear skies and long historical runways all combined to make it a fun place to fly. Over the years, however, the air base at Wendover had gradually deteriorated due to time, vandalism and inaction." To help preserve this historic site, Jim founded *Historic Wendover Airfield*, a private tax-exempt foundation dedicated to preserving the World War II buildings and history of the site. He and a dedicated group of volunteers are now hard at work preserving this history.

A mess hall that really hasn't changed all that much from its WW II days. If only its walls could speak!

163

Above: Volunteers hard at work painting the Squadron Operations Building. (PETERSEN)

Today's view of two assembly buildings that are located in the Technical Area. Here the components of the test atom bombs were assembled. The building on the left is the one in which Leon Smith worked on the radar systems that were part of the Fat Man fusing system. The building on the right was used for assembly work on both Fat Man and Little Boy. (PETERSEN)

Looking up at a hangar roof gives a nice view of the wood construction. The wood is still in excellent condition today. (PETERSEN)

One of the more interesting projects for the preservationists was to clean one of the four pits used to load two types of atomic bombs into the specially modified B-29s. The pit had not been used since World War II, and as a result was a resting place for about two feet of dirt, rocks, and other debris. During the cleaning, about 40 rounds

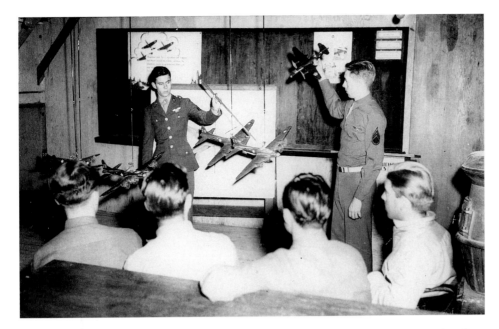

Class in session. Apparently a class on formation flying showing the protective fire gained from other aircraft in the formation while under attack. (PETERSEN)

The author's daughter standing in front of one of the former WW II hangars.

of .50 caliber ammunition were found, some still linked together. The "find" was turned over to the Air Force. Another interesting project is the restoration of the bomb sight storage building. This large building still has the 10' by 40' storage vault used to safeguard the Norden bombsights. The vault has 5 separate storage compartments each guarded by a Diebold vault door. At one time, the building also had a rather extensive air conditioning and heating system that was backed up by an auxiliary power system.

One of the more difficult and expensive restoration efforts was the repair of the roof of the building known as the Enola Gay hangar, which housed some of the B-29s of the 509th Bombardment group during their stay at Wendover. Today, this massive building needs major repair work. The roof was a significant start.

Other preservation projects are in progress around the field which will help insure that this part of our national heritage is here for future generations. Additional funds are urgently needed to ensure the preservation work continues. The Historic Wendover Group has put together an attractive package of benefits for those who choose to make a donation to continue the preservation efforts. The group can be reached at www.wendoverairbase.com.

Appendix: USAAF Airfields

FIELD OR AIRSTRIP	MILES FROM NEAREST TOWN	FIELD OR AIRSTRIP	MILES FROM NEAREST TOWN
Eagle Field	6 mi. SW Dos Palos	San Nicolas Army Air Field	75 mi. SW Los Angeles
Estrella Army Air Field	5 mi. NE Paso Robles	Santa Maria Army Air Field	4 mi. S Santa Maria
Eureka Navy Airport	14 mi. N Eureka	Santa Rosa Army Air Field	7 mi. NW Santa Rosa
Fairfield-Suisun Army Air Field	5 mi. E Fairfield	Shaver's Summitt Field	30 mi. ESE Indio
Gardner Field	8 mi. E Gardner	Siskiyou County Field	5 mi. NE Montaque
Grand Central Air Terminal		Stockton Field	4 mi. SSE Stockton
(March Field, sub base)	6 mi. NW Glendale	Thermal Army Air Field	2 mi. SW Thermal
Half Moon Bay Flight Strip	5 mi. NW Half Moon Bay	Victorville Army Air Field	5 mi. NW Victorville
Hamilton Field	7 mi. NNE San Rafiel	Visalia Army Air Field	6 mi. W Visalia
Hammer Field	5 mi. NE Fresno	Willows Airfield	
Hayward Army Air Field	3 mi. W Hayward	(Hamilton Field, aux.)	1 mi. W Willows
Hawthorne Field	1 mi. E Hawthorne	Winters Flight Strip	7 mi. NE Winters
Kern (Gardner Field, aux.)	21 mi. SE Taft	Van Nuys Metro Airport	17 mi. NW Los Angeles
Kern County Field	1 mi. WNW Inyokern		
Kern County Field	5 mi. NNW Bakersfield		
Kearney-Mesa Airport	8 mi. NE San Diego	COLORADO	
King City Field	2 mi. NNE King City		
Lemoore Army Air Field	9 mi. SW Lemoore	Arlington (La Junta, aux.)	28 mi. NNE Arlington
Lindbergh	2 mi. W San Diego	Buckley Field	8 mi. SE Denver
Lomita Flight Strip	1 mi. W Lomita	Denver Municipal Airport	5 mi. ENE Denver
Long Beach Army Air Field (ATC)	4 mi. NE Long Beach	La Junta Army Air Field	4 mi. NNE La Junta
Los Angeles Field	11 mi. SW Los Angeles	Las Animas (La Junta, aux.)	19 mi. NE La Junta
Lost Hills-Kern County	1 mi. NE Lost Hills	Leadville Flight Strip	2 mi. W Leadville
March Field	10 mi. SE Riverside	Lowry Field	1 mi. SE Denver
Marysville Army Air Field	3 mi. S Marysville	Peterson Field	7 mi. ESE Colorado Springs
Mather Field	10 mi. E Sacramento		
M C Flight Test Base	20 mi. SE Mojave	Pueblo Army Air Base	7 mi. ENE Pueblo
McClellan Field	8 mi. NE Sacramento	Pueblo Field	2 mi. SW Pueblo
Merced Army Air Field	6 mi. NW Merced	Rocky Ford (La Junta, aux.)	14 mi. NW La Junta
Merced Air Base (Merced AAF, aux.)	2 mi. NW Merced		
Metropolitan Airport	2 mi. NW Van Nuys		
Mills Field	10 mi. S San Francisco	CONNECTICUT	
Mines Field	10 mi. SW Los Angeles		
Minter Field	14 mi. NW Bakersfield	Bradley Field	2 mi. W Windsor Locks
Modesto Field	2 mi. ESE Modesto	Brainard Field	2 mi. SSE Hartford
Montague Airfield	3 mi. NE Montague	Bridgeport Army Air Field	3 mi. SE Stratford
Muroc Army Air Field	1 mi. S Muroc	Groton Army Air Field	3 mi. SE Groton
Muroc Flight Test Base	3 mi. N Muroc	New Haven Army Air Field	3 mi. SE New Haven
Napa Airfield	5 mi. S Napa	Rentschler Field	3 mi. ESE Hartford
Needles Army Airfield	5 mi. S Needles		
Oakland Municipal Airport		DELAWARE	
(Hamilton Field, sub base)	5 mi. S Oakland		
Ontario Army Air Field	1 mi. E Ontario	Dover Army Air Field	4 mi. SE Dover
Orange County Army Air Field	4 mi. S Santa Ana	New Castle Army Air Base	5 mi. SW Wilmington
Oroville Army Air Field	3 mi. SW Oroville		
Otay-Mesa NAAS	14 mi. SE San Diego		
Oxnard Flight Strip	6 mi. E. Oxnard	FLORIDA	
Palmdale Army Air Field	3 mi. NE Palmdale		
Palm Springs Army Air Field	2 mi. E Palm Springs	Alachua Army Air Field	3 mi. NE Gainesville
Parker (Gardner Field aux.)	15 mi. SE Taft	Apalachicola Army Air Field	8 mi. W Apalachicola
Potterville Army Air Field	3 mi. SW Potterville	Avon Park Army Air Field	10 mi. ENE Avon Park
Ream Field (March Field, aux.)	12 mi. S San Diego	Bartow Army Air Field	5 mi. NE Bartow
Redding Army Air Field	7 mi. SE Redding	Boca Raton Army Air Field	2 mi. NW Boca Raton
Rice Army Air Field	2 mi. ESE Rice	Brooksville Army Air Field	4 mi. S Brooksville
Sacramento Municipal Airport		Buckingham Army Air Field	4 mi. E Fort Myers
(Hamilton Field, sub base)	5 mi. S Sacramento	Bushnell Army Air Field	3 mi. NE Bushnell
Salinas Army Air Base	3 mi. SE Salinas	Carrabelle Flight Strip	2 mi. W Carrabelle
San Bernardino Army Air Depot	3 mi. ESE San Bernardino	Cross City Army Air Field	1 mi. E Cross City
San Diego Municipal Airport	1 mi. W San Diego	Dale Mabry Field	2 mi. WSW Tallahassee
San Diego Naval Air Station	North Island		

FIELD OR AIRSTRIP	MILES FROM NEAREST TOWN	FIELD OR AIRSTRIP	MILES FROM NEAREST TOWN
Drew Field	5 mi. W Tampa	Daniel Field	3 mi. WSW Augusta
Dunnellon Army Air	5 mi. E Dunnellon	Dublin Airfield	5 mi. NW Dublin
Eglin Field	2 mi. W Valpariso	Harris Neck Army Air Field	7 mi. ES Newport
Eglin aux. #1	14 mi. NNE Valpariso	Herbert Smart Airport	4 mi. E Macon
Eglin aux. #2	6 mi. NNE Valpariso	Homerville Flight Strip	2 mi. NW Homerville
Eglin aux. #3	10 mi. N Valpariso	Hunter Field	3 mi. SW Savannah
Eglin aux. #4	6 mi. W Valpariso	Lake Park Field (Moody Field, aux.)	12 mi. SSE Valdosta
Eglin aux. #5	10 mi. NW Valpariso	Lawson Field	8 mi. S Columbus
Eglin aux. #6	18 mi. WNW Valpariso	Marietta Army Air Field	2 mi. SE Marietta
Eglin aux. #7	19 mi. W Valpariso	Moody Field	23 mi. NE Valdosta
Eglin aux. #8	10 mi. ENE Valpariso	Moultrie Field	7 mi. S Moultrie
Eglin aux. #9	14 mi. WSW Valpariso	Robins Field	17 mi. SE Macon
Hendricks Field	5 mi. SE Sebring	Spence Field	4 mi. SE Moultrie
Hillsborough Army Air Field	6 mi. NNW Tampa	Statesboro Army Air Field	3 mi. NE Statesboro
Homestead Army Air Field	5 mi. ENE Homestead	Sylvania Army Air Field	7 mi. SSE Sylvania
Immokalee Airfield	1 mi. NE Immokalee	Thomasville Army Air Field	8 mi. NE Thomasville
Jacksonville Army Air Field	6 mi. N Jacksonville	Tifton Field	2 mi. SE Tifton
Keystone Army Air Field	3 mi. NNW Keystone Heights	Turner Field	3 mi. E Albany
		Valdosta Field	2 mi. S Valdosta
Kissimmee Army Air Field	2 mi. N Kissimmee	Vidalia Airfield	3 mi. SE Vidalia
Lakeland Army Air Field	3 mi. N Lakeland	Waycross Army Air Field	3 mi. NW Waycross
Lake Wales Airfield	2 mi. WSW Lake Wales		
Leesburg Army Air Field	5 mi. E Leesburg		
Leesburg Base Services	7 mi. NW Leesburg	**IDAHO**	
Mac Dill Field	8 mi. SSW Tampa		
Marathon Flight Strip	3 mi. ENE Marathon	Gowen Field	3 mi. S Boise
Marianna Army Air Field	6 mi. NNE Marianna	Mountain Home Army Air Base	11 mi. WSW Mountain Home
Montbrook Army Air Field	2 mi. NW Montbrook		
Morrison Field	2 mi. SW Palm Beach	Pocatello Army Air Field	8 mi. NW Pocatello
Naples Army Air Field	1 mi. NE Naples	Pocatello Field	6 mi. NW Pocatello
Orlando Air Base	2 mi. E Orlando		
Page Field	4 mi. S Fort Myers		
Palm Beach County Park	2 mi. WNW Lantana	**ILLINOIS**	
Pan American 36th St., Army Air Base	6 mi. NW Miami	Chanute Field	1 mi. S Rantoul
Perry Army Air Field	3 mi. S Perry	Chicago Municipal Airport	8 mi. SW Loop District
Pinecastle Army Air Field	7 mi. SE Pinecastle	Curtiss-Steinberg	4 mi. SSW East St. Louis
Pinellas Army Air Field	10 mi. N St. Petersburg	George Field	4 mi. NE Lawrenceville
Prospect Field (Boca Raton AAF, aux.)	1 mi. WNW Boca Raton	Orchard Place Airport	14 mi. NW Chicago
Punta Gorda Army Air Field	4 mi. ESE Punta Gorda	Presbyterian Church aux. #3	4 mi. WNW Lawrenceville
Sarasota Army Air Field	4 mi. NNW Sarasota	Scott Field	9 mi. NE Belleville
Taylor Field	1 mi. SW Ocala	St. Charles Field	3 mi. E St. Charles
Tyndall Field	8 mi. SE Panama City		
Venice Army Air Field	Venice	**INDIANA**	
Zephyrhills Army Air Field	1 mi. SE Zephyrhills		
		Atterbury Army Air Field	3 mi. N Columbus
GEORGIA		Baer Field	5 mi. SW Fort Wayne
		Bendix Field	3 mi. NW South Bend
Adel Field	2 mi. W Adel	Emison (George Field, aux.)	4 mi. WSW Oaktown
Atlanta Municipal Airport	8 mi. S Atlanta	Evansville Municipal Airport	5 mi. NE Evansville
Bush Field	8 mi. SSE Augusta	Freeman Field	2 mi. S Seymour
Bainbridge Army Air Field	4 mi. NNW Bainbridge	Madison Army Air Field	5 mi. NNW Madison
Bemis Field (Moody Field, aux.)	12 mi. NE Valdosta	St. Anne (Freeman Field, aux.)	2 mi. NNE North Vernon
Camp Stewart Army Air Field	3 mi. NE Hinesville	Stout Field	5 mi. SW Indianapolis
Chatham Army Air Field	6 mi. NW Savannah	Walesboro Field (Freeman Field, aux.)	1 mi. WSW Walesboro
Cochran Field	9 mi. S Macon		
Commodre Decatur Field	2 mi. W Bainbridge		
Cordele Field	2 mi. NNE Cordele		

FIELD OR AIRSTRIP	MILES FROM NEAREST TOWN	FIELD OR AIRSTRIP	MILES FROM NEAREST TOWN

IOWA

Burlington Field	2 mi. SSW Burlington
Des Moines Field	3 mi. SSW Des Moines
Sioux City Army Air Base	6 mi. SSE Sioux City

KANSAS

Atkinson Field	3 mi. NW Pittsburg
Coffeyville Army Air Field	5 mi. NNW Coffeyville
Coffeyville AAF aux. #3	16 mi. ENE Coffeyville
Coffeyville Field	2 mi. NW Coffeyville
Dodge City Army Air Field	5 mi. WNW Dodge City
Dodge City Field	3 mi. ENE Dodge City
Dodge City aux. #4	17 mi. NNE Dodge City
Fairfax Field	1 mi. N Kansas City
Garden City Army Air Field	9 mi. ESE Garden City
Garden City AAF aux. #1	19 mi. ESE Garden City
Garden City AAF aux. #2	13 mi. E Garden City
Garden City AAF aux. #3	6 mi. ENE Garden City
Great Bend Army Air Field	5 mi. W Great Bend
Herington Army Air Field	6 mi. E Herington
Independence Army Air Field	6 mi. SW Independence
Independence AAF aux. #9	12 mi. NE Independence
Liberal Army Air Field	2 mi. W Liberal
Marshall Field	2 mi. SE Fort Riley
Phillip Billard	4 mi. ENE Topeka
Pratt Army Air Field	5 mi. N Pratt
Sherman Field	1 mi. NNE Fort Leavenworth
Smoky Hill Army Air Field	5 mi. SW Salina
South Field aux. #5	4 mi. W Arkansas City
Strother Field	5 mi. SSW Winfield
Topeka Army Air Field	7 mi. S Topeka
Walker Army Air Field	1 mi. E Walker
Wichita Municipal Airport	5 mi. SE Wichita

KENTUCKY

Bowman Field	5 mi. E Louisville
Campbell Army Air Field	13 mi. NW Clarksville
Godman Field	Fort Knox
Lexington AFS	5 mi. W Lexington
Standiford Field	6 mi. SE Louisville
Paducah Municipal Airport (Nashville, aux.)	Paducah
Sturgis Army Air Field	1 mi. E Sturgis

LOUISIANA

Alexandria Army Air Field	6 mi. WNW Alexandria
Alvin Callender	8 mi. SSE New Orleans
Barksdale Field	6 mi. E Shreveport
DeRidder Army Air Base	3 mi. WSW DeRidder
Esler Field	10 mi. NE Alexandria
Hammond Army Air Field	3 mi. E Hammond
Harding Field	5 mi. N Baton Rouge

Lafayette Field	1 mi. SE Lafayette
Lake Charles Army Air Field	3 mi. ESE Lake Charles
Leesville Landing Strip	2 mi. NW Leesville
Mansfield Airfield	4 mi. NW Mansfield
Natchitoches Field	1 mi. SSW Natchitoches
New Orleans Army Air Base	6 mi. NE New Orleans
Pollock Army Air Base	4 mi. SW Pollock
Selman Field	2 mi. NW Monroe
Shreveport Field	2 mi. NNE Shreveport

MAINE

Deblois Flight Strip	2 mi. SE Deblois
Dow Field	2 mi. W Bangor
Houlton Army Air Field	2 mi. E Houlton
Pittsfield Field	1 mi. SSE Pittsfield
Presque Isle Army Air Field	2 mi. WNW Presque Isle

MARYLAND

Baltimore Army Air Field	6 mi. SE Baltimore
Edgewood Arsenal	1 mi. S Edgewood Arsenal
Fort Meade	Fort Meade
Martin Field (Baltimore AAF aux.)	10 mi. NE Baltimore
Phillips Field	5 mi. SE Aberdeen
Salisbury Airfield	1 mi. NE Salisbury
Salisbury Field #2	5 mi. ESE Salisbury

MASSACHUSETTS

Barnes Airport	3 mi. NNE Westfield
New Bedford Army Air Field	2 mi. SE Bedford
Boston Municipal Airport	4 mi. E Boston
Fort Devens Army Air Field	1 mi. NW Avers
Hyannis Airfield	1 mi. N Hyannis
New Bedford Army Air Field	2 mi. NW New Bedford
Otis Field	8 mi. NE Falmouth
Westover Field	4 mi. NE Chicopee

MICHIGAN

Alpena Army Air Field	7 mi. WNW Alpena
Detroit City Field	6 mi. NE Detroit
Grayling Army Air Field	1 mi. NW Grayling
Kalamazoo Field	4 mi. SSE Kalamazoo
Kellogg Field	3 mi. WSW Battle Creek
Kent County Field	4 mi. SSE Grand Rapids
Muskegon Field	5 mi. S Muskegon
Oscoda Army Air Field	4 mi. NW Oscoda
Romulus Army Air Field	16 mi. SW Detroit
Selfridge Field	3 mi. E Mt. Clemens
Tri-City Army Air Field	10 mi. NW Saginaw
Willow Run Airport	3 mi. E Ypsilanti

MINNESOTA

Camp Ripley Field	7 mi. N Little Falls
Flyn Field (Glider Training)	12 mi. E St. Paul
Minneapolis Field (Chamberlain)	6 mi. SSE Minneapolis
Rochester Municipal Airport	1 mi. SE Rochester
St. Paul Municipal Airport	2 mi. SE St. Paul

MISSISSIPPI

Hancock County Bombing Range	9 mi. NW Bay St. Louis
Columbus Army Air Field	10 mi. NNW Columbus
Greenville Army Air Field	8 mi. NE Greenville
Greenville-Washington County Field	2 mi. E Greenville
Greenwood Army Air Field	6 mi. SE Greenwood
Greenwood Field	2 mi. SW Greenwood
Grenada Army Air Field	4 mi. NE Grenada
Gulfport Army Air Field	3 mi. NE Gulfport
Gulfport Field	1 mi. N Gulfport
Hancock County Airport	8 mi. NW Bay St. Louis
Hinds County (Jackson AB aux.)	13 mi. W Jackson
Hattiesburg Army Air Field	4 mi. SE Hattiesburg
Jackson Air Base	3 mi. NW Jackson
Keesler Field	2 mi. W Biloxi
Key Field	3 mi. SW Meridian
Laurel Army Air Field	3 mi. SW Laurel
Lime Prairie Field (Jackson AAB aux.)	30 mi. ENE Jackson

MISSOURI

Chester Field	4 mi. NW McBride
Columbia Field	2 mi. NW Columbia
Deblois Flight Strip	2 mi. S Deblois
Dexter AAF (aux. #1)	1 mi. SSE Dexter
Fort Leonard Wood	SW corner
Gideon AAF (aux. #4)	1 mi. SE Gideon
Jefferson Barracks	10 mi. SW St. Louis
Joplin Field	5 mi. NNE Joplin
Kansas City Municipal Airport	1 mi. N Kansas City
Lambert Field	11 mi. NW St. Louis
Malden Army Air Field	2 mi. NNW Malden
Rosecrans Field	4 mi. NW St. Joseph
Sedalia Army Air Field	2 mi. S Knobnoster
Vichy Army Air Field	12 mi. W Rolla

MONTANA

Cut Bank Army Air Field	2 mi. SW Cut Bank
Dell Flight Strip	1 mi. NW Dell
Glasgow Army Air Field	3 mi. N Glasgow
Gore Field	3 mi. WSW Great Falls
Great Falls Army Air Field	4 mi. E Great Falls
Helena Field	3 mi. ENE Helena
Lewistown Army Air Field	1 mi. WSW Lewistown

NEBRASKA

Ainsworth Army Air Field	5 mi. W Ainsworth
Alliance Army Air Field	5 mi. SE Alliance
Bruning Army Air Field	8 mi. E Bruning
Fairmont Army Air Field	2 mi. S Fairmont
Grand Island Army Air Field	2 mi. NNE Grand Island
Grand Island (aux.)	2 mi. NE Grand Island
Harvard Army Air Field	2 mi. N Harvard
Kearney Army Air Field	1 mi. E Kearney
Lee Bird Field	3 mi. ESE North Platte
Lincoln Army Air Field	7 mi. NW Lincoln
McCook Army Air Field	7 mi. NNW McCook
Offutt Field	9 mi. S Omaha
Omaha Field	3 mi. NE Omaha
Scottsbluff Army Air Field	3 mi. E Scottsbluff
Scribner Army Air Field	2 mi. S Scribner
Union Field	5 mi. NNE Lincoln

NEVADA

Caliente Flight Strip	21 mi. W Caliente
Camp Raleigh Field	2 mi. S Camp Raleigh
Freeman Field	5 mi. SE Fallon
Indian Springs Army Air Field	1 mi. N Indian Springs
Lahontan Flight Strip	15 mi. S Fernley
Las Vegas Army Air Field	7 mi. NE Las Vegas
Las Vegas Airfield	6 mi. NE Las Vegas
Owyhee Flight Strip	4 mi. W Owyhee
Reno Army Air Base	10 mi. NNW Reno
Tonopah Army Air Field	8 mi. E Tonopah
Tonopah (aux. #5)	44 mi. SE Tonopah

NEW HAMPSHIRE

Claremont Field	1 mi. W Claremont
Concord Field	1 mi. ENE Concord
Grenier Field	4 mi. S Manchester
Nashua Field	3 mi. WNW Nashua
Portsmouth Airfield	3 mi. W Portsmouth

NEW JERSEY

Bendix Airport	Bendix
Caldwell-Wright Field	2 mi. N Caldwell
Fort Dix Army Air Base	1 mi. SW Wrightstown
Milleville Army Air Field	3 mi. SW Milleville
Moorestown Field	2 mi. NNE Moorestown
Newark Army Air Field	2 mi. S Newark
Fort Dix Army Air Base	1 mi. SE Wrightstown

NEW MEXICO

Alamogordo Army Air Field	9 mi. WSW Alamogordo
Albuquerque Army Air Field	3 mi. S Albuquerque
Camp Luna	7 mi. NW Las Vegas
Carlsbad Army Air Field	2 mi. S Carlsbad
Carlsbad AAF (aux. #1)	10 mi. S Carlsbad
Clovis Army Air Field	5 mi. W Clovis
Crews Field	12 mi. SSW Raton
Deming Army Air Field	2 mi. E Deming
Deming AAF (aux. #1)	19 mi. SSW Deming
Deming AAF (aux. #2)	11 mi. W Deming
Fort Sumner Army Air Field	1 mi. E Fort Sumner
Fort Sumner AAF (aux. #5)	16 mi. ENE Fort Sumner
Hobbs Army Air Field	4 mi. NW Hobbs
Kirtland Field	3 mi. SSE Albuquerque
Roswell Army Air Field	7 mi. S Roswell
Roswell AAF (aux. #1)	8 mi. SW Roswell
Santa Fe Army Air Field	10 mi. WSW Santa Fe

NEW YORK

Albany Field	7 mi. NNW Albany
Buffalo Municipal Airport	8 mi. ENE Buffalo
Elizabeth Field	West end of Fisher's Island
Farmingdale Army Air Field	1 mi. E Farmingdale
Idlewild Airfield	13 mi. SE New York
LaGuardia Field	5 mi. E New York
Mastic Flight Strip	2 mi. NW Mastic
Mitchel Field	1 mi. NE Hempstead
Montgomery Field (USMA aux. #1)	2 mi. SW Montgomery
New Hackensack (USMA aux. #3)	1 mi. W New Hackensack
Niagara Falls Field	4 mi. E Niagara Falls
Niagara Municipal Airport	6 mi. SW Niagara Falls
Rome Army Air Field	2 mi. ENE Rome
Rome Flight Strip	26 mi. S Rome
Roosevelt NAF	2 mi. ESE Mineola
Stewart Field	8 mi. NNW Newburgh
Suffolk County Army Air Field	1 mi. NE Westhampton Beach
Syracuse Field	6 mi. WNW Syracuse
Wallkill (UAMA aux. #2)	3 mi. NW Wallkill
Watertown Field	6 mi. NW Watertown
Wheeler-Sack Field	11 mi. ENE Watertown
Westchester County Airport	4 mi. NE White Plains

NORTH CAROLINA

Ashville-Hendersonville Field	12 mi. SSE Ashville
Barco Flight Strip	2 mi. W Barco
Bluethenthal Field	3 mi. NE Wilmington
Camp Davis Army Air Field	1 mi. NNE Hollyridge
Camp Mackall Field	4 mi. E Hoffman
Charlotte Municipal Field	6 mi. W Charlotte
Fairchild Aircraft Field	2 mi. E Burlington
Balloon Field (aux. #1)	1 mi. NNW Fort Bragg
Greensboro Municipal Airport	8 mi. W Greensboro
Lumberton Field #2 (Gliders)	3 mi. WSW Lumberton

Hoffman (Camp Mackall)	4 mi. NE Hoffman
Laurinburg-Maxton Army Air Base	2 mi. N Maxton
Morris Field	5 mi. WSW Charlotte
Pope Field	12 mi. NW Fayetteville
Raleigh Durham Army Air Field	11 mi. NW Raleigh Durham
Smith-Reynolds Airport	2 mi. N Winston-Salem
Seymour Johnson Field	3 mi. SE Goldsboro

NORTH DAKOTA

Bismarck Municipal Airport	2 mi. SE Bismarck
Fargo Municipal Airport	2 mi. NW Fargo

OHIO

Cleveland Municipal Airport	9 mi. SW Cleveland
Clinton County Army Air Field	1 mi. E Wilmington
Dayton Municipal Airport	12 mi. N Dayton
Lockbourne Army Air Field	9 mi. S Columbus
Lunken Airport	4 mi. E Cincinnati
Middletown Field	1 mi. N Middletown
Patterson Field	10 mi. SE Dayton
Toledo Field	7 mi. SSE Toledo
Wright Field	5 mi. E Dayton

OKLAHOMA

Altus Army Air Field	2 mi. ENE Altus
Ardmore Army Air Field	9 mi. N Ardmore
Bethany Field #2	8 mi. WNW Oklahoma City
Enid Army Air Field	5 mi. SSW Enid
Frederick Army Air Field	2 mi. SE Frederick
Gage Airfield (Will Rogers Field aux.)	2 mi. SSW Gage
Great Salt Plains Bombing Range	5 mi. NE Jet
Hobart Airfield	3 mi. SE Hobart
Miami Field	2 mi. NNW Miami
Muskogee Airport	2 mi. W Muskogee
Muskogee Army Air Field (Will Rogers Field S.B.)	5 mi. S Muskogee
Perry Airfield	6 mi. N Perry
Ponca City Field	3 mi. NNW Ponca City
Tinker Field	9 mi. SE Oklahoma City
Tulsa Field	6 mi. NE Tulsa
Tulsa AAF	7 mi. ENE Tulsa
Will Rogers Field	7 mi. SW Oklahoma City
Woodring Field	5 mi. ESE Enid
Woodward Army Air Field	7 mi. W Woodward

OREGON

Alkali Lake Flight Strip	14 mi. SW Wagontire
Aurora Flight Strip	1 mi. NW Aurora
Boardman Flight Strip	5 mi. WSW Boardman
Corvallis Army Air Field	2 mi. S Corvallis

Field or Airstrip	Miles from Nearest Town
Eugene Municipal Airport	7 mi. NW Eugene
Hillsboro Municipal Airport	2 mi. NE Hillsboro
Madris Army Air Field	2 mi. NNW Madris
Mahlon Sweet Field	8 mi. NW Eugene
McMinnville Airfield	3 mi. ESE McMinnville
Medford Army Air Field	2 mi. N Medford
Pendleton Field	3 mi. NW Pendleton
Portland Army Air Base	6 mi. NNE Portland
Redmond Army Air Field	1 mi. ESE Redmond
Rome Flight Strip	27 mi. SW Rome
Salem Army Air Field	1 mi. SE Salem
The Dalles Field	2 mi. NE The Dalles

PENNSYLVANIA

Field or Airstrip	Miles from Nearest Town
Connellsville Municipal Airport	5 mi. SW Connellsville
Harrisburg Municipal Airport	4 mi. S Harrisburg
Olmstead Field	1 mi. W Middletown
Philadelphia Municipal Airport	6 mi. SW Philadelphia
Pittsburg-Allegheny County Airport	7 mi. SE Pittsburgh
Reading Army Air Field	3 mi. NW Reading
Waynesboro Municipal Airport	3 mi. SE Waynesboro
Williamsport Field	4 mi. E Williamsport

RHODE ISLAND

Field or Airstrip	Miles from Nearest Town
Hillsgrove Army Air Field	5 mi. S Providence

SOUTH CAROLINA

Field or Airstrip	Miles from Nearest Town
Aiken Army Air Field	7 mi. NNE Aiken
Anderson Airfield (Greenville AAB aux.)	3 mi. W Anderson
Barnwell Airfield (Columbia AAB aux.)	2 mi. NW Barnwell
Charlestown Army Air Field	10 mi. NW Charlestown
Chester Airfield	6 mi. NNE Chester
Columbia Army Air Base	6 mi. SW Columbia
Congaree Army Air Field	15 mi. ESE Columbia
Coranca Army Air Field	4 mi. N Greenwood
Florence Army Air Field	2 mi. ESE Florence
Greenville Army Air Base	7 mi. SSE Greenville
Greenville Municipal Airport	3 mi. E Greenville
Hartsfield Airfield (Greenville AAB aux.)	3 mi. N Hartsfield
Johns Island Airfield (Columbia AAB aux.)	7 mi. SSW Charlestown
Myrtle Beach Army Air Field	3 mi. WSW Myrtle Beach
North Airfield	1 mi. ESE North
Ocean Drive Flight Strip	3 mi. WSW Ocean Drive
Owens Field	3 mi. SE Columbia
Shaw Field	7 mi. NW Sumter
Spartanburg Airfield	2 mi. SSW Spartanburg
Walterboro Army Air Field	2 mi. NE Walterboro
Wampee Flight Strip	3 mi. S Wampee

SOUTH DAKOTA

Field or Airstrip	Miles from Nearest Town
Mitchell Army Air Field	4 mi. N Mitchell
Pierre Army Air Field	4 mi. ENE Pierre
Rapid City Army Air Base	9 mi. NE Rapid City
Sioux Falls Army Air Field	3 mi. NE Sioux Falls
Watertown Army Air Field	2 mi. NW Watertown

TENNESSEE

Field or Airstrip	Miles from Nearest Town
Berry Field	6 mi. SE Nashville
Dyersburg Army Air Field	12 mi. S Dyersburg
McKeller Field	5 mi. W Jackson
Memphis Municipal Airport	8 mi. SE Memphis
Smyrna Army Air Field	1 mi. N Smyrna
Tri-City Field	12 mi. NNW Tri-City
Wm. Nothern Field	2 mi. NW Tullahoma

TEXAS

Field or Airstrip	Miles from Nearest Town
Abernathy Field	6 mi. E Abernathy
Abilene Air Terminal	3 mi. ESE Abilene
Abilene Army Air Field	7 mi. WSW Abilene
Alamo Field	7 mi. NNE San Antonio
Aloe Army Air Field	4 mi. WSW Victoria
Aloe AAF (aux. #10)	20 mi. WSW Victoria
Amarillo Army Air Field	9 mi. ENE Amarillo
Amarillo Field	6 mi. ENE Amarillo
Avenger Field	4 mi. W Sweetwater
Bergstrom Field	8 mi. E Austin
Biggs Field	8 mi. NE El Paso
Big Spring Army Air Field	3 mi. W Big Spring
Big Spring Army Glider School	18 mi. NNW Big Spring
Biggs Field	6 mi. NE El Paso
Blackland Army Air Field	3 mi. W Big Spring
Brooks Field	3 mi. SSE San Antonio
Brownsville Municipal Airport	5 mi. E Brownsville
Brownwood Army Air Field	5 mi. NNE Brownwood
Bryan Army Air Field	5 mi. SW Bryan
Childress Army Air Field	3 mi. W Childress
Cox Field	5 mi. ESE Paris
Dalhart Army Air Field	3 mi. SSW Dalhart
Dalhart Sub Base #1	10 mi. W Dalhart
Dalhart Sub Base #2	11 mi. NE Dalhart
Dyche Field	9 mi. SW Fort Stockton
Eagle Pass Army Air Field	10 mi. NE Eagle Pass
Ellington Field	12 mi. SE Houston
Ellington aux. #2	3 mi. WNW Houston
El Paso Municipal Airport	5 mi. ENE El Paso
Fort Worth Army Air Field	7 mi. WNW Fort Worth
Foster Field	5 mi. NE Victoria
Foster aux. #4	13 mi. NNW Victoria
Gainsville Army Air Field	3 mi. WNW Gainsville
Galveston Army Air Field	5 mi. SW Galveston
Gaskin Field (Perrin Field aux.)	13 mi. SW Sherman
Gibbs Field	2 mi. NNW Fort Stockton
Goodfellow Field	3 mi. SE San Angelo
Harlingen Army Air Field	3 mi. NE Harlingen

References

CHAPTER ONE

Brown, Charles, Major AUS (Ret.). *Black Field Artillery Pilots of World War II.*

Davis, Benjamin O. Jr., Gen. U.S.A.F. (Ret.). *Benjamin O. Davis, Jr. American,* Smithsonian Institution Press, Washington/London, 1991.

Francis, Charles. *The Tuskegee Airmen,* Bruce Humphries Inc., Boston, 1955.

Homan, Lynn and Thomas Reilly. *The Tuskegee Airmen,* Arcadia Publishing Co., Charleston, South Carolina, 1998.

Holton, William. *The Tuskegee Airmen Story (A Speech Guide),* East Coast Chapter, Tuskegee Airmen, Inc., 1977.

Rose, Robert D.D.S. *Lonely Eagles,* Tuskegee Airmen Inc., Los Angeles Chapter, Los Angeles, California, 1976.

Sandler, Stanley. *Segregated Skies,* Smithsonian Institution Press, Washington/London, 1992.

Station History, Tuskegee Army Air Field, U.S.A.F. Historical Research Center, Maxwell AFB, Alabama.

_____, *The Hawks Cry,* base newspaper, Tuskegee Army Air Field.

_____, *The Tuskegee News,* Tuskegee Alabama, various articles, 1942–1948.

_____, *The Pittsburgh Courier,* Pittsburgh, Pennsylvania, various articles 1941– 1946.

Wreckhorst, Donald. *75 year Pictorial History of Chanute Air Force Base Rantoul Illinois,* Evangel Press, Nappanee, Illinois, 1992.

Conversations/correspondence: Dr.and Mrs.Caesar Bassette, Mr. Herbert Carter, Mr. C. Rodney Custis, Mr. and Mrs. Charles Dunn, Mr. Ed (Don) Doram, Dr. Lawrence Hawkins, Mr. John Leahr, Col. Roosevelt Lewis U.SA.F. (Ret.), Mr. David McPheeters, Mr. Nick Neblett, Mr. Godfrey Miller, and Dr. Julian Peasant.

CHAPTER TWO

Craven, Wesley, and James Cate. *The Army Air Forces in World War II, Vol. VI,* the University of Chicago Press, 1955.

Fahey, James. *U.S. Army Aircraft 1908-1946* Ships and Aircraft, Falls Church, VA, 1946.

Granger, Byrd. *On Final Approach,* Falconer Publishing Co., Scottsdale AZ, 1991

Hickman, Ivan. *Operation Pinball,* Motorbooks International, Osceola WI, 1990.

Larkins, William. *Kingman Army Air Field,* Arizona, Aerophile, Vol.2 Number 1, 1947.

Thole, Lou. *Forgotten Fields of America, Vol. II,* Pictorial Histories Publishing Co. Inc., Missoula, MT 1999.

_____ *Descriptions of Airports and Landing Fields In The United States,* Airway Bulletin No. 2, United States Government Printing Office, Washington, DC, 1938.

Mohave County Miner, various articles, Kingman, AZ, 1941–1947.

Station History, Kingman Army Air Field, U.S.A.F. Historical Research Center, Maxwell AFB, AL.

_____ *The Cactus,* base newspaper, Kingman Army Air Field, 1944.

Freeman, Roger, *Airfields of the Eighth Then and Now,* Battle of Britain Prints International Ltd., London, England, 1978.

Conversations/correspondence: Mr. Norman Berge, Mr. John Hoza, Mrs. Lenore Hafley, and Mr. Richard Schneider

CHAPTER THREE

Bentley, Blair. Dr. *Dyersburg Army Air Base,* Dyersburg State Gazette, articles, July 6, 1990 and June 18, 1990, Dyersburg, Tennessee.

Craven and Cate. *The Army Air Forces In World War II,* Vol. Six, University of Chicago Press, Chicago, Illinois, 1955.

Fahey, James. *U.S. Army Aircraft, 1908–1946,* Ships and Aircraft, Falls Church, Virginia, 1964.

Thole, Lou. *Forgotten Fields Of America,* Volume II, Pictorial Histories Inc., Missoula, Montana, 1999.

Dyersburg State Gazette, various articles 1942–1945. Dyersburg, Tennessee.

Janes Fighting Aircraft of World War II, Military Press, New York, NY New York, 1989.

Station History, Dyersburg Army Air Field, Air Force Historical Research Center, Maxwell AFB, Alabama.

Station History, Walnut Ridge Army Air Field, Air Force Historical Research Center, Maxwell AFB, Alabama.

Vox Prop, base newspaper, Dyersburg Army Air Field.

_____ *Aircraft Accidents in the Continental U.S. December 1941 to August 1945*, headquarters United States Air Force History Support Office, Bolling AFB, Washington, D.C.

Conversations/correspondence: Mr. Tim Bivens, Mrs. Pat Higdon, Mr. Sonny Higdon, Mr. John Barnacle, Mr. Cecil Caudill, Mr. Clause (Hoot) Watkins, Mr. Ken Otto, Mr. Harold Brown, Mr. Wayne Ferguson

CHAPTER FOUR

Craven, Crate. *The Army Air Forces in World War II*, Vol. II, Men and Planes, The University of Chicago Press, Chicago, Illinois 1955.

Mauer, Mauer. *World War II Combat Squadrons of The United States Air Force*, U.S.A.F. Historical Division, Smithmark Publishers, Inc., New York, N.Y. 1992.

Sarasota Herald-Tribune, Sarasota, Florida, various articles, 1941–1946.

Station History, Venice Army Air Field, U.S.A.F. Historical Research Agency, Maxwell AFB, Alabama.

Venice Aerial, Venice Army Air Field newspaper.

Conversations/Correspondence: Mr. John Becket, Ms. Adele Cohill, Mr. Bill Guyton, Ms. Dorothy Korwek, Mr. Harry Lee, Ms. Christa Lim, Mr. Mack Pong

CHAPTER FIVE

Birdsall, Steve. *Log of the Liberators*, Doubleday & Company, Inc., Garden City, New York, 1973.

Board, Purdy, and Esther Colcord. *A History of Aviation in Lee County, Florida, 1983.*

Cameron, Rebecca. *Training To Fly, Military Flight Training, 1909–1945*, Air Force History and Museums Program, 1999.

Fahey, James. *U.S. Army Aircraft, Ships and Aircraft*, Falls Church Virginia, Reprint 1964.

Maurer, Maurer. *Air Force Combat Units of World War II*, Office of Air Force History, Washington, D.C., 1983.

_____ *Fighter Flashes*, base newspaper, Page Field, March 21, 1945.

_____ *Fort Myers News Press*, Fort Myers, Florida, various articles, 1942.

History of Page Field, U.S.A.F Historical Research Center, Maxwell AFB, Alabama.

Conversations/Correspondence: Mr. John Becket, Mr. Art Ferwerda, Mr. Tom Griffin, Mr. James Hinkle, Mr. Paul London, Mr. Stanley Mulsford, Mr. Dean Reno.

CHAPTER SIX

Ammerman, Gale. *An American Glider Pilot's Story*, Merriam Press, Bennington, Vermont, 2001

Devlin, Gerard. *Silent Wings*, St. Martins Press, New York, N.Y., 1985

Fahey, James. *U.S. Army Aircraft 1908–1946*, Ships and aircraft, Falls Church, VA, 1964.

Lowden, John. *Silent Wings At War*, Smithsonian Institute Press, Washington and London, 1992.

Maurer Maurer. *Air Force Combat Units of World War II*, Office of Air Force History, Washington, D.C., 1983.

Thole, Lou. *Forgotten Fields of America. Vol. I*, Pictorial Histories Publishing Co., Inc., Missoula, Montana, 1996.

Base History, Laurinburg-Maxton Army Air Base, USAF Historical Research Agency, Maxwell AFB, Alabama.

Colliers Encyclopedia, The Crowell Publishing Company, 1962.

The Laurinburg Exchange, Laurinburg North Carolina, various issues, 1942-1946.

The Slipstream, base newspaper, Laurinburg-Maxton Army Air Base, various issues.

The Hamlet News Messenger, December 2, 1943, Hamlet, North Carolina.

_____ *On Tow*, National World War II Glider Pilots Association, Fort Pierce, Florida, 1990.

Conversations/Correspondence: Ms. Pat Hamer, Dr. Winston Turnow, Mr. Charles Anderson, Mr. George Theis, Mr. Tom MacCallum, Mr. Gale Ammerman, Mr. Vern Ward, Ms. Lille McKay, Mr. Bob Sanford, Mr. Randy Hoffman, Mr. John Mc Rae, Brig. General Clinton Willis, Jr., USA, (Ret.) Mr. Larry Barnett, Ms Ann Slaughter.

CHAPTER SEVEN

Bodie, Warren. *The Lockheed P-38 Lightning*, Widewing Publications, Hiawassee, Georgia, 1991.

Bone, Walt. *"Air Jeep" Wings*, Sentry Magazine, Inc. New York, New York, February 1974.

Craven, Wesley, and James Cate. *The Army Air Forces In World War II, Vol. VI, Men And Planes*, The University of Chicago Press, Chicago, Illinois, 1955.

Thole, Lou. *Forgotten Fields of America Vol. I*, Pictorial Histories Publishing Co., Missoula, Montana, 1996.

Army Air Forces Station List, Buildings and Grounds Section, HQ. Army Air Forces, Washington, D.C., 4 November 1943.

Chandler Arizonan. various articles, 1941–1945.

University of Arizona Bulletin, Chapter VI, *The War Years, 1941-1945*.

Williams Field, Base History, USAF Historical Research Agency, Maxwell AFB, Montgomery, Alabama.

_____ *Willy Field Happenings During World War (Believe Them or Not)*, 1983

U. S. Army Aircraft 1908–1946, Ships And Aircraft, Falls Church, Virginia, 1946.

Authors note: I want to thank Tom Kelly for the time and help he gave me while researching and writing this chapter. His help was considerable and was motivated by the love and respect he has for his Dad. His father was an instructor pilot on aircraft such as the B-17, B-29 and B-36. Part of his time in the Air Force was spent at Williams Air Force Base as an instrument instructor pilot on the B-17.

CHAPTER EIGHT

Craven, Wesley, and James Cate. *The Army Air Forces in World War II, Vol. VI Men and Planes*, University of Chicago Press, Chicago, Illinois 1955.

Correl, John. *Air Force Magazine*, 2002 USAF Almanac, May 2002, Arlington VA.

Donald, David. *The Complete Encyclopedia of World Aircraft*, Barnes & Noble Inc., New York, N. Y., 1997.

Fahey, James. *U.S. Army Aircraft, 1908–1946*, Ships and Aircraft, Falls Church VA, 1946.

Hill, Mike, and John Cambell, and Donna Cambell. *Peace Was Their Profession SAC A Tribute*, Schiffer Military/Aviation History, Atglen PA, 1995

McDermott, Kate, and Sherry Medders. *A History Covering The 50 Years of Columbus Air Force Base, 1941–1991*, Columbus AFB Public Affairs Office, 1991.

Warnken, Pam, Editor, and Alexis Lloyd. Public Affairs, *Silver Wings*, base newspaper Columbus Air Force Base, various editions 2002.)

_____ *A Brief History of Columbus AFB and the 14th Flying Training Wing*, Office of History, HQ 14th Flying Training Wing, Columbus AFB, Mississippi, 2000.

Aircraft Accidents in the Continental US—Numbers and Rate December 1941 to August 1945, Office of Flying Safety, History Support Office, Bolling AFB, Washington, D.C.

Flight Manual U.S.A.F. Services T-37 B Aircraft, SA-ALC Automated Technical Order System, Change7 —7August 2000.

Station History, Columbus Army Air Field, USAF Historical Research Center, Maxwell AFB, Alabama.

Student Pilot Handbook, 14th Flying Training Wing, Columbus Air Force Base, 1 July 2002.

_____ *The Official Guide to the Army Air Forces*, Pocket Books Inc., New York, N.Y. 1944.

Fact Sheet, T-1A Jayhawk, Air Education and Training Command, Randolph, Randolph AFB, Texas, May 2002.

14th Flying Training Wing, SUPT Inprocessing Checklist—Columbus Air Force Base, 1 July 2002

Conversations/correspondence: Lt. Joseph Coslett, SS Kyle Ford, Mr.Brent Green, Lt. Shannon Hodge, Ms. Connie Lisowski, Lt. Col. PJ McLauglin USAF (Ret.) Lt. Jennifer Moore, SS Brent Ochs, Lt. John Poole, Lt. Col. Robert Schultz USAF (Ret.), Captain Timothy Sundvall, Major David Thole, Col. Thomas Quelly, Lt. Ryan Venhuizen, and Ms.Pamela Warnken.

CHAPTER NINE

Beckman Joseph Rev. Letters to his parents, February 27 to June 1, 1944.

Fahey, James. *U.S. Army Aircraft 1908–1946*, Ships and Aircraft, Falls Church VA, 1964

Mauer, Mauer. *Air Force Combat Units of World II*, Office of Air Force History, Washington, D.C., 1983.

Mauer, Mauer. *World War II Combat Squadrons of the United States Air Force*, USAF Historical Division, Air University, Smithmark Publishers Inc., New York, NY, 1992.

Metscher, Allen. correspondence with various Tonopah AAF veterans.

Army Air Forces Station List, 4 November 1943, Headquarters Army Air Forces, Washington, D.C.

Central Nevada's Glorious Past, a publication of the Central Nevada Historical Society, Various articles by Kay Carpenter, John Darr, Beverly Duffy, Allen Metscher, Vernon Nightengale, Warren Roquet, and Western Construction News.

Technically Speaking, Carter& Burgess, Inc., Denver CO, 2001.

Tonopah AAF, Base History, Air Force Historical Research Agency, Maxwell AFB, Alabama.

Tonopah Daily Times Bonanza, various articles 1940-1948.

Conversations/Correspondence: Rev. Joe Beckman, Kay Carpenter, Allen Metscher, Merle Olmsted, and Chuck Yeager.

Chapter Ten

Army Air Forces Station List, HQ. Army Air Forces, Washington D.C., November 1943.

Inactivation Ceremony for 64th Flying Training Wing (pamphlet) Reese Air Force Base, 30 September 1997.

Lubbock Texas, *Avalanche Journal*, various articles, 1997

Memorialisation Program, Reese Air Force Base, Air Force Museum, WPAFB, Ohio

Conversations/correspondence: Ms. C. Diane Bailey, Mr. Joe Don Buckner, Mr. Les Clemmons, Mr. Alan Henry, Mr. Lyle Hopkins, Ms. Bobbie Morelle, Mr. Bill Tynan.

Chapter Eleven

Arrington, Leonard, and Thomas Alexander. *Worlds largest Military Reserve: Wendover Air Force Base,* 1941–63, Utah Historical Quarterly, Vol. 31, NO. 4, Fall 1963.

Arrington, Leonard, Thomas Alexander, and Charles Hubbard. *World War II Activities,* and *Post War History*, Historic Wendover Airbase Restoration, 2002.

Craven, W., and Cate, J. *The Army Air Forces In World War II, Vol. VI, Men and Planes*, University of Chicago Press, Chicago Illinois, 1955.

Johnson, Barbara. *A Brief History of Wendover Airport*, FAA, December 1990.

Rowe, James. *Project W-47*, Ja A Ro publishing, Livermore, California, 1978.

Thole, Lou. *Forgotten Fields of America, Vol.II*, Pictorial Histories Publishing Company, Inc. Missoula Montana, 1999.

_____ *Brief History of Wendover Air Force Base-1940-1946*, USAF Historical Researches Studies Institute, Maxwell AFB, Alabama, July 1956.

_____ *History of Wendover Air Force Base, Part II, Temporary Buildings*, U.S.Air Force Legal Office, Hill Air Force Base, Ogden, Utah

Station History, Wendover Air Force Base, USAAF Historical Research Center, Maxwell AFB, Alabama.

Conversations/correspondence: Mr. Chris Melville, Dr. Donald Klinko, Mr. James Petersen, and Mr. Thomas Petersen.

Appendix

This information is taken from the *Army Air Forces Station List, 4 November 1943* and the *U.S. Army and Navy Directory of Airfields (Continental United States) February 1, 1944*. The author attempted to list every significant field used in any capacity by the USAF during that period. Not listed are primary training fields, and many grass landing strips that had no significant use. Since the number of airfields and landing strips was constantly changing during the war (dependent upon training needs) some fields may have been deleted or not listed.

About the Author

Lou Thole has written two previous books along with many aviation articles, most of which focus on World War II, USAAF training fields. He is a noted aviation historian, whose work has been published in newspapers and magazines including the *Friends Journal* (the publication of the Air Force Museum) and *FlyPast*. A retired sales manager, he holds a private pilot license and a glider rating. Lou lives in Cincinnati, Ohio, with his wife, Jane. They are the parents of three children.